INEQUALITY
AT THE
STARTING GATE

Other books from the

ECONOMIC POLICY INSTITUTE

The State of Working America

School Vouchers:
Examining the Evidence

The Class Size Debate

Can Public Schools Learn From Private Schools?

Where's the Money Gone?
Changes in the Level and Composition of Education Spending

Risky Business:
Private Management of Public Schools

School Choice:
Examining the Evidence

INEQUALITY AT THE STARTING GATE

◆

Social Background Differences in Achievement as Children Begin School

Valerie E. Lee and David T. Burkam
UNIVERSITY OF MICHIGAN

ECONOMIC POLICY INSTITUTE

Washington, D.C.

ECONOMIC POLICY INSTITUTE
1660 L Street, NW, Suite 1200
Washington, D.C. 20036

http://www.epinet.org

ISBN:1-932066-02-0

Table of contents

About the authors

Valerie E. Lee is a professor of education at the University of Michigan, where she teaches courses in quantitative methods, sociology of education, and program evaluation. She holds master's and doctoral degrees in education from Harvard University and a bachelor's in chemistry from Stanford University. Dr. Lee also taught math and science in elementary secondary schools in the U.S., France, and Abu Dhabi. Virtually all her research has focused on issues of educational equity, with an emphasis on programmatic elements that simultaneously increase both student learning and its equitable distribution by race, social class, and gender. Her most recent book is *Restructuring High Schools for Equity and Excellence: What Works?* (2001). She is also a co-author of *Catholic Schools and the Common Good* (1993), as well as many journal articles and reports.

David T. Burkam is a lecturer and an assistant research scientist at the University of Michigan, where he has joint appointment spanning the school of education and the residential college. He earned his bachelor's degree from Wittenberg University and his master's and doctoral degrees from the University of Michigan. He teaches research methods and design, program evaluation, freshmen writing, quantitative reasoning, and sociology of education. Dr. Burkam is the author of many articles and reports, and his recent research includes equity issues in kindergarten and early schooling; gender equity in math and science; high school curriculum structure; and measurement issues in student course-taking and achievement. He received the 2001 Residential College Excellence in Teaching Award and was cited for creating interdisciplinary courses that bridge the gap between mathematics, the social sciences, and the humanities.

Executive Summary

A key goal of education is to make sure that every student has a chance to excel, both in school and in life. Increasingly, children's success in school determines their success as adults, determining whether and where they go to college, what professions that enter, and how much they are paid.

There are many factors preventing education from serving this role as "the great equalizer." Schools serving low-income students receive fewer resources, face greater difficulties attracting qualified teachers, face many more challenges in addressing student's needs, and receive less support from parents. This inequality of school quality is widely recognized.

But the inequalities facing children before they enter school are less publicized. We should expect schools to increase achievement for all students, regardless of race, income, class, and prior achievement. But it is unreasonable to expect schools to completely eliminate any large pre-existing inequalities soon after children first enter the education system, especially if those schools are under-funded and over-challenged.

This report shows that the inequalities of children's cognitive ability are substantial right from "the starting gate." Disadvantaged children start kindergarten with significantly lower cognitive skills than their more advantaged counterparts. These same disadvantaged children are then placed in low-resource schools, magnifying the initial inequality.

These conclusions are based on analysis of the U.S. Department of Education's Early Childhood Longitudinal Study, Kindergarten Cohort (ECLS-K)—a recent and comprehensive data collection effort that provides a nationally representative picture of kindergarten students. We report observed differences in young children's achievement scores in literacy and mathematics by race, ethnicity, and socioeconomic status (SES) as they begin kindergarten. We also explore differences by social background in a wide array of children's family and home conditions

and activities. Our analysis leads to several conclusions relevant for education policy, including:

- There are substantial differences by race and ethnicity in children's test scores as they begin kindergarten. Before even entering kindergarten, the average cognitive score of children in the highest SES group are 60% above the scores of the lowest SES group. Moreover, average math achievement is 21% lower for black than for whites, and 19% lower for Hispanics.

- Race and ethnicity are associated with SES. For example, 34% of black children and 29% of Hispanic children are in the lowest quintile of SES compared with only 9% of white children. Cognitive skills are much less closely related to race/ethnicity after accounting for SES. Even after taking race differences into account, however, children from different SES groups achieve at different levels.

- Family structure and educational expectations have important associations with SES, race/ethnicity, and with young children's test scores, though their impacts on cognitive skills are much smaller than either race or SES. Although 15% of white children live with only one parent, 54% of black and 27% of Hispanic children live in single-parent homes. Similarly, 48% of families in the lowest SES quintile are headed by a single parent, compared to only 10% of families in the highest quintile.

- Socioeconomic status is quite strongly related to cognitive skills. Of the many categories of factors considered—including race/ethnicity, family educational expectations, access to quality child care, home reading, computer use, and television habits—SES accounts for more of the unique variation in cognitive scores than any other factor by far. Entering race/ethnic differences are substantially explained by these other factors; SES differences are reduced but remain sizeable.

- Low-SES children begin school at kindergarten in systematically lower-quality elementary schools than their more advantaged counterparts. However school quality is defined—in terms of higher student achievement, more school resources, more qualified teachers, more positive teacher attitudes, better neighborhood or school conditions, private vs. public schools—the least advantaged U.S. children

begin their formal schooling in consistently lower-quality schools. This reinforces the inequalities that develop even before children reach school age.

These new data are some of the most detailed ever collected for the study of children's characteristics as they enter kindergarten. And the results are clear—disadvantaged children fall behind at a very early age, before they ever enter a classroom. Schools must be held accountable for raising achievement for all students, but this may not eliminate initial inequalities. However, initial inequalities should not be magnified by the schooling process.

There is also some evidence in the report about how these initial inequalities can be reduced. Children who attended center-based preschool arrive at kindergarten with higher achievement, providing the potential to reduce inequality by the time students reach kindergarten. Also, reducing the inequality of school resources, which this study clearly documents, would aid in reducing the inequality that children and schools face at the starting gate.

Introduction

Inequality at School Entry

Americans' beliefs about education are inconsistent. We recognize, on the one hand, that children neither begin nor end their education on an equal footing. On the other hand, Americans simultaneously believe that schools are places where social inequalities should be equalized, where the advantages or disadvantages that children experience in their homes and families should not determine what happens to them in school—in essence, that school is a place where children should have equal chances to make the most of their potential. There is widespread faith among Americans in the value of education for social betterment, for both individuals and the nation. Among the many institutions in U.S. society, schooling is seen by most Americans as the embodiment of meritocracy. They believe—or at least hope—that children's experiences in our nation's elementary and secondary schools allow them to succeed without regard to their family circumstances, their race or ethnicity, or their gender.

Despite widespread faith in the role of schooling to address or ameliorate social inequalities, we should recognize that our nation's schools actually play a major role in magnifying such inequalities. For example, it is common knowledge that children's school performance, including scores on standardized tests of academic achievement, is associated with their family background, particularly race, ethnicity, and socioeconomic status. Several social scientists have written about how schools structure inequality, so that social differences in achievement actually increase as a result of children's participation in differentiated educational experiences as they move through school.

The focus of this report is inequality. We explore social differences in academic competence among young children at the point at which they begin school. As many researchers have noted, the need to document and understand these differences has become increasingly clear in recent years:

Two important indicators of success of a society are the level of literacy of its children and youth, and the extent of disparities in literacy skills among children and youth with differing characteristics and family backgrounds. These indicators are markers of how investments of material, social and cultural resources made during the past decade have been translated into skills and competencies in the present generation: they denote the success of families, schools, and communities in producing a literate society. (Willms 1999, 72)

Rather than targeting their educational experiences in school, this report centers on social differentiation in children's cognitive status at the point where they arrive at the schoolhouse door. Young children do not begin school as equals. Although many children have informal educational experiences early in their lives—in preschool, Head Start, or child care—kindergarten is the point where virtually all children begin their formal education. Although the age when children enroll in kindergarten is close to constant (typically, 5 years old), their cognitive status when they begin kindergarten varies considerably. Unfortunately, this status, which might be measured with appropriate tests of skills and knowledge, is associated with family background. In this report we use the U.S. government's most current and nationally representative data, the *Early Childhood Longitudinal Study, Kindergarten Cohort*, to explore how American children's social background (particularly race, ethnicity, and socioeconomic status, or SES) is linked with their cognitive status as they all embark on their formal school experience.

Relevant Theory and Research

Risk factors for school failure. Children's early experiences in school represent an "especially critical but generally neglected period in research on child development" (Alexander and Entwistle 1989, 1). Among those who do investigate early schooling, there is considerable and long-standing debate about whether social background differences in school performance are a result of "cultural deprivation" (also called "social deprivation") or "educational deprivation" (Natriello, McDill, and Pallas 1990). Current language that has considerable support among educational sociologists includes descriptors such as "at risk" and "educational disadvantage."

But casting the debate in these terms may actually inhibit individuals from fulfilling their potential (Fantini and Weinstein 1968). Factors defining risk or educational disadvantage include race and ethnicity, poverty,

single-parent family structure, poorly educated mothers, and limited English proficiency (Natriello et al. 1990). Although a study of Baltimore school children found few race differences in children's performance at entry into first grade (Entwisle, Alexander, and Olson 1997), other research using data from the National Assessment for Educational Progress (NAEP) has documented substantial differences by race for elementary school children (e.g., Applebee et al. 1988), and at least one study documents substantial cognitive differences between black and white children at as early as three and four years old (Jencks and Phillips 1998). Natriello et al. (1990) estimate that about 40% of school-age children are "at risk."

Although other researchers estimate slightly lower proportions—and there is some disagreement about exactly what factors constitute risk— virtually all agree that the proportion of the school population that is at risk of school failure is growing. Although large numbers of children have trouble learning to read, such difficulties are much more likely to occur among poor children, non-white children, and non-native speakers of English (Snow, Burns, and Griffin 1998). Virtually all researchers agree that social background factors are associated with school success. Moreover, there is general agreement that social stratification in educational outcomes increases as children move through school (Entwisle et al. 1997; Phillips, Crouse, and Ralph 1998).[1] Social inequalities in school increase as children advance through school mainly because of differentiation in educational experiences that begin as early as first grade (with reading groups, special education placement, and retention), extend through elementary school (as ability grouping, special education, and gifted and talented programs continue), and are well recognized by high school (with formal and informal tracking, advanced placement, and the like).

Despite many studies that have resulted in widespread agreement that social background influences children's educational experiences and successes, the association between family background and cognitive performance at the point where children *enter* school has received less empirical scrutiny. Many studies have evaluated the efficacy of preschool programs designed to enhance the cognitive and social competence of disadvantaged children (such as Head Start and state-financed preschool programs for low-income children). Many other studies have targeted the experiences of children in elementary school who have already demonstrated educational problems.

Social background and young children's development. A few carefully designed studies have focused on very young children's development of language skills (e.g., Hart and Risley 1995; Huttenlocher, Haight, Bryk,

and Seltzer 1991). Such studies often require repeated and regular observations in children's homes to investigate family dynamics that are associated with infants' and toddlers' vocabulary development. These studies demonstrate quite conclusively that mothers' speech (its frequency, elaboration, and verbal interchanges with children) is closely linked to young children's vocabulary development. Moreover, early vocabulary development is strongly associated with later school performance. One study, in which researchers observed mother-child interactions every month for the first two years of children's lives, concluded that the elaboration of mothers' language interactions with their young children was strongly differentiated by social class (Hart and Risley 1995). Moreover, socially linked language development observed in very young children was found to be quite stable throughout elementary school (i.e., schooling did not ameliorate these socially based language differences developed in infancy). Intergenerational transmission of language was substantial.

Socioeconomic gradients for children and youth. Several relevant articles in a recent international and multidisciplinary volume explore the strength and variation in socioeconomic gradients, or slopes (e.g., Brooks-Gunn, Duncan, and Britto 1999; Case, Griffin, and Kelly 1999; Willms 1999). Case et al. explore SES differences in numerical competency that emerge at the same time that differences in biological and/or neurological development lead to differential higher-order cognitive functioning. Using international data, Willms observes that countries with high average literacy scores among youth tend to have shallow gradients, that is, youth from lower socioeconomic backgrounds also demonstrate relatively high literacy. Furthermore, he offers additional evidence to support the essential link between SES effects and context (including family, community, and schools) that results from "segregating low-status groups from mainstream society…by their place of residence in most cities worldwide" (Willms 1999, 90).

Brooks-Gunn and her colleagues found certain large (albeit selective) associations between family income and children's attainment:

> Most noteworthy is the importance of the type of outcome being considered. Family income has large effects on some of the children's ability and achievement measures, but large effects on none of the behavior, mental health, or physical health measures represented by the dozen developmental studies (1999, 107).

Moreover, they contend that very poor children are especially disadvantaged, far more than children at or just above the poverty threshold.

Two especially relevant studies. A recent study by Phillips, Brooks-Gunn, Duncan, Klebenov, and Crane (1998) is particularly relevant to the research in this report. There are three similarities between this report and theirs: (1) both focus on children of about the same age, (2) both examine how children's cognitive performance is associated with social background, (3) both aim to explain the link between social background and cognitive performance by other family factors. Although Phillips and her colleagues (1998) used different data and different measures of family background, they examined the magnitudes of black/white test-score gaps on two different measures of cognitive performance for 5- and 6-year-olds and how those gaps were influenced by taking into account measures of family background (including that of grandparents), parents' attitudes and behaviors, and mothers' IQ and school performance. Initial score differences by race were greatly reduced when these factors were controlled. The study described in this report takes a similar approach.

A study by Stipek and Ryan (1997) is also especially relevant to this report, mostly in terms of the first two of the three similarities shared with the Phillips et al. (1998) study. A difference from the study by Phillips and colleagues is that the Stipek and Ryan study focused on the social background factor of SES instead of race. However, besides examining cognitive performance as children begin kindergarten, these researchers explored such outcomes as performance gain, self-confidence, attitudes toward school, expectations for success, and preference for challenge. Although economically disadvantaged children scored lower on initial cognitive performance, SES-related differences remained steady over the first two years of school. Moreover, there were few differences related to disadvantage on other outcomes.

How the Report is Organized

As the title implies, this report is about social inequality. We focus on children who are at risk for school failure, based on several aspects of their social backgrounds (particularly race and social class[2]). However, instead of focusing on schooling per se, we target children at an important stage of their intellectual and social development: the point at which all of them begin their formal schooling in kindergarten. We make use of an important new source of data on a nationally representative sample of kindergarten children to examine how social disadvantage is associated with cognitive skills in reading and mathematics. Our organization of the report around young children's performance on standardized tests of academic achieve-

ment suggests its important connection to education, although we do not explore children's experience or performance in school. The report is organized into five chapters, and although none is tied directly to children's experiences in school, the analysis in each successive chapter moves closer to school. The chapters build on one another, and analyses in successive chapters also become somewhat more complex analytically.

Chapter 1, which is descriptive, examines the magnitude of social background differences in cognitive skills, as well as the association between race and social class among these children. Chapter 2 links social background to other aspects of family demographic characteristics and behavior. Chapter 3 examines whether (and how) the link between social background and cognitive status may be "explained" by taking into account the aspects of children's family behaviors and demographic characteristics explored in the previous chapter. This approach is similar to that taken by Phillips, Brooks-Gunn, and their colleagues (1998). Chapter 4 comes closer to considering schooling and investigates how children are mapped to the types of elementary schools where they attend kindergarten, based again on their social backgrounds. In particular, we define the schools according to an array of school quality indicators. In Chapter 5, we discuss possible implications of our results for social policy.

CHAPTER 1

Social and academic disadvantage as children enter kindergarten

The aim of this chapter is to provide descriptive information about how children from different social backgrounds score on tests of cognitive status in reading and mathematics as they begin kindergarten. We define social background in terms of children's race, ethnicity, and socioeconomic status (SES).

Details of analyses

The data source. The U.S. Department of Education recently undertook a major new data collection effort that allows us to explore these questions in depth. In 1998 the Department of Education began a nationally representative longitudinal study of young children—the Early Childhood Longitudinal Study, Kindergarten Cohort (ECLS-K)—that starts when they entered kindergarten. In a nationally representative sample of about 1,000 U.S. public and private schools that offer kindergarten, the ECLS-K study team randomly selected about 25 kindergartners in each school. Although the ECLS-K sample of children was meant to be random, children whose understanding of English (the language of testing) was below an established cut score on a brief language screener were not tested.[3] All children whose native language was English and those who passed the language screening were tested one-on-one by trained professionals, in a non-timed setting, in reading (or literacy) and mathematics near the beginning of their kindergarten year.

One of each child's parents (typically the mother) also completed an extensive survey, as did his or her kindergarten teacher and an administrator (usually the principal) in the child's school. However, because this study's focus is on children as they begin school, the information used in this report is mostly drawn from over 16,000 children with test scores and whose parents provided full information about race, ethnicity, and socioeconomic status.

In Chapter 4 we explore how children's social background is associated with the quality of the elementary schools they attend. We drew much of our information about school quality from the surveys completed by school administrators and teachers. Although the study is longitudinal, meaning that the same children are tested (and their parents and teachers interviewed) at several timepoints, this report's focus is on "the educational starting gate," that is, when children begin kindergarten. Many of the analyses make use of composite variables that we have constructed from individual items included in the first-wave ECLS-K data file. For readers interested in this level of detail, or those who may wish to make use of these valuable data to replicate or expand on our results, we provide information about the construction of all variables used in this report, including the actual ECLS-K items from which composite measures were constructed, in the Appendix. ECLS-K data are available from the National Center for Education Statistics (NCES) free of charge.[4]

The tests. The ECLS-K reading test in kindergarten assesses children's basic literacy skills, which include recognizing printed words, identifying sounds, vocabulary, word reading, and reading comprehension (NCES 2000a). This test of reading skills administered to kindergartners refers to children's emergent literacy, phonemic knowledge, and language development. These skills include understandings that print has meaning, as well as children's oral language and receptive vocabulary (Snow et al. 1998). The ECLS-K test of mathematical knowledge assesses the operations and processes needed for problem solving and reasoning with numbers. The skills on the ECLS-K battery "include, but are not limited to, the understanding of the properties of numbers, mathematical operations (e.g., addition), and problem solving. They also include understanding the patterns and relationships of numbers, formulating conjectures, and identifying solutions" (NCES 2000a, 11).

The test scores in both reading and mathematics were equated with Item Response Theory (IRT) scaling methods. "IRT uses the pattern of right, wrong, and omitted responses to items actually administered in a test and the difficulty, discriminating ability, and the 'guess-ability' of each item to place each child on a continuous ability scale" (NCES 2000b, 3-2). There is a substantial advantage of using IRT-scaled scores: they estimate the score a child *would have achieved* if all of the items on all forms of the test had been administered. Although not directly relevant to this report, the use of IRT scoring also makes possible the longitudinal measurement of achievement gain over time. This is extremely important in a longitudinal study such as ECLS-K.

Analysis strategy. The ECLS-K dataset follows a nested structure, with children sampled from the schools they entered. Normally, any multivariate analyses using data with such a structure need to make use of statistical methods that take nesting into account.[5] However, because our focus is not on what happens to children in school but rather on their status as they present themselves at school entry, we argue that our analyses need not take this multilevel data structure into account. This allows us to use, as our major multivariate analysis method, ordinary least-squares (OLS) regression. Throughout the report our focus is on differences by race, ethnicity, and SES in children's cognitive achievement in reading and mathematics at kindergarten entry. Analyses in Chapters 1 and 2 are descriptive. We make use of multivariate methods (mostly OLS regression) in Chapters 3 and 4.

A major advantage of ECLS-K is that it is nationally representative. However, the sampling design of ECLS-K included intentional over-sampling of children in private schools and Asian/Pacific Islanders. To adjust for this over-sampling and for non-response, our analyses throughout this report make use of the child-level design weights supplied by ECLS-K.[6] Using these weights allows us to generalize our results to the U.S. population of children who entered kindergarten in fall 1998.

Results in effect sizes. We have chosen to present many of the results throughout the report in effect-size (or standard deviation [SD]) units— using z-scored versions of these tests (mean=0, pooled standard deviation=1)—for three reasons. First, effect-size units facilitate comparisons across tests and social groups. Second, these units allow readers to consider what is important beyond the rather arbitrary standards of statistical significance (which are influenced by sample sizes). Third, this way of presenting results has become increasingly common in the worlds of social policy and program evaluation. In most instances we focus on magnitudes of effect sizes rather than their statistical significance. With large sample sizes, such as those in ECLS-K, even very small differences or effects are often statistically significant.

How would readers know whether a particular effect size were big or small? A commonly used set of standards is presented by Rosenthal and Rosnow (1984), who describe effect sizes at or above .5 SD as "large," .3-.5 SD as "moderate," .1-.3 SD as "small," and those below .1 SD as "trivial." Results of federally mandated impact evaluations that assess program effects of social and educational intervention are now quite commonly presented in effect-size units (GAO 2001). In a meta-analysis of studies assessing the impact of Head Start (called The Head Start Synthesis Project)

published almost two decades earlier, when effect sizes were less commonly used than now, the authors provided another and perhaps more substantive interpretation of effect sizes:

> Educators and researchers in early childhood education commonly consider an effect size in the range of 0.25 or greater (either positive or negative) to be educational meaningful. Differences of this size accompany noticeable improvements in classroom performance (McKey et al. 1985, 5).

However, both the GAO report (2001) and the Head Start Synthesis Project (McKey et al. 1985) were using these units to quantify effects of children's participation in some social intervention, compared to a reasonable standard. This study is not an evaluation of any particular educational intervention, but rather describes social differences in the population of U.S. children who began kindergarten in 1998. Thus, a standard of "educational significance" may not apply here. We remind readers that all the differences we present in this report are comparisons (for race/ethnicity, comparisons are with white children; for SES, we present our results in quintiles in comparison to the middle quintile). We hope that the standards we provide for judging whether effects are small or large may be useful in interpreting the results presented here. We present many of our results in graphic form, so the patterns of associations are clearer than they often are in tables.

Were we considering gains in achievement over a single school year (such as kindergarten), we would be in a good position to discuss a more meaningful standard: learning. In other research we have conducted using ECLS-K (Lee, Burkam, Honigman, and Meisels 2001), we evaluated the effects of a social intervention in terms of "months of learning" (i.e., how much achievement the average kindergarten child in the U.S. would be expected to gain in one month in the school year). However, because in this report our focus is on children's scores on these tests at a single time point (i.e., our research is cross-sectional rather than longitudinal), we believe that effect size is the most appropriate metric to consider.

Descriptive findings about social background and cognitive status

Racial/ethnic composition of America's kindergarten class of 1998. This report describes a nationally representative sample of U.S. children who

FIGURE 1.1 Kindergartners by race

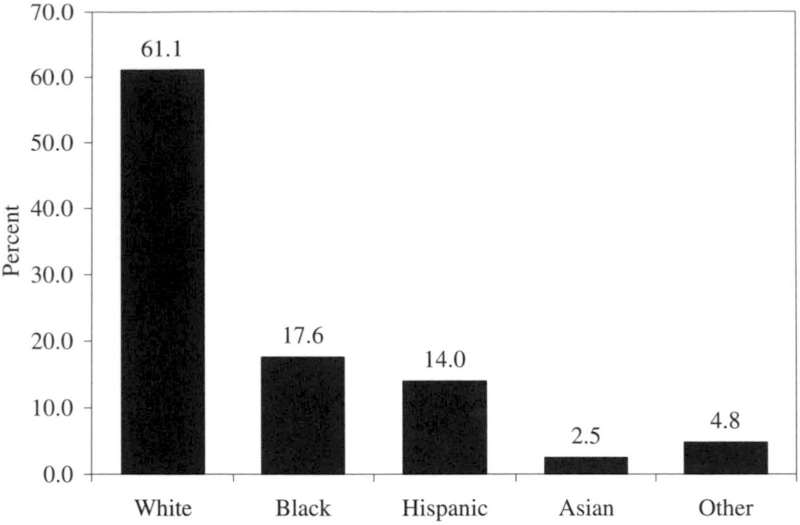

Source: Authors' analysis of U.S. Department of Education ECLS-K data.

began kindergarten in the fall of 1998. The racial/ethnic breakdown of America's kindergartners in that year, displayed in **Figure 1.1**, is as follows: 61.1% of incoming kindergartners in 1998 were white, 17.6% were black, 14.0% were Hispanic, 2.5% were Asian, and 4.8% were classified as "other." About half of the "other" group came from mixed-race families (50.5% of that 4.8%), and 38.8% were Native Americans (including Alaskan natives). The remainder (10.7%) were native Hawaiians. We use the four racial/ethnic groups—black, Hispanic, Asian, and other—for most of the analyses in this report. In analyses where we include comparisons among racial groups, the comparison group is whites.[7] The association between racial/ethnic group membership and SES is explored later in this chapter.

Race and ethnicity—differences in beginning achievement. **Figure 1.2** displays test-score averages in mathematics and reading for children from different racial/ethnic groups (panel A indicates actual scores, panel B indicates group differences in effect-size units). White and Asian children's scores on these tests are similar (panel A), and consistently higher than those for black, Hispanic, and other children. Recall that most children in

**FIGURE 1.2   Math and reading achievement at the beginning
of kindergarten**

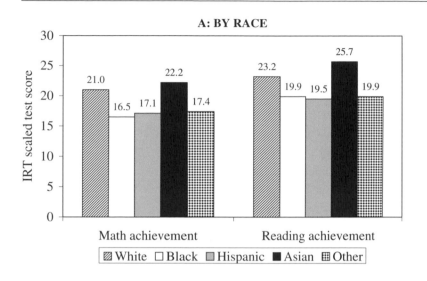

A: BY RACE

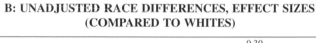

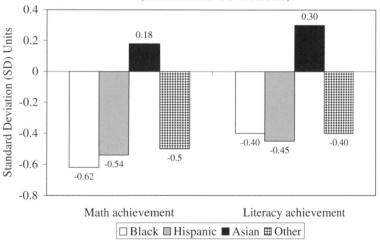

B: UNADJUSTED RACE DIFFERENCES, EFFECT SIZES
(COMPARED TO WHITES)

Source: Authors' analysis of U.S. Department of Education ECLS-K data.

the "other" category are either Native American or biracial (i.e., their parents indicated more than one racial category on the survey). White and Asian children outscore blacks, Hispanics, and other children by four to five points on the tests in both subjects. There are smaller differences among black, Hispanic, and other children, and between white and Asian children.

Another way to display these differences is in effect sizes, shown in panel B of Figure 1.2. The effects displayed here are in score differences (in standard deviation [SD] units), with each racial/ethnic group mean compared to the mean for the largest group, white children. Examined this way, several trends are clear. First, black, Hispanic, and children in the "other" racial group score about one-half SD below their white counterparts, whereas Asian children score somewhat above whites. Second, the effect size differences are generally larger for mathematics (on the left) than for reading (on the right). Racial/ethnic differences are large (.5 SD or more) for mathematics, moderate (.3-.5 SD) for reading (see endnote 1). Third, black/white differences are largest in mathematics (an effect size of -.62 SD), whereas Hispanic/white differences are largest in reading (-.45 SD), even though Hispanic children with very weak English skills were not tested. Fourth, Asian children outscore whites more in reading than in mathematics at entry into kindergarten. This may seem surprising, except that Asian children with limited English skills were not tested (see endnote 3).

Differences in beginning achievement status by SES. **Figure 1.3** displays differences on these same tests by socioeconomic status. Readers should keep in mind that it is standard procedure in social science research to measure socioeconomic status as a composite score that includes parents' reports of their household income, mothers' and fathers' education, and mothers' and fathers' occupation (scored on an occupational prestige scale drawn from the 1989 General Social Survey—NCES 2000b). Although it might be useful to explore these issues using each component of SES, we have chosen to use the composite SES measure for the sake of brevity. Here we divided children into five groups (i.e., quintiles) of approximately equal size (20% in each quintile), based on their SES. In panel A of Figure 1.2, a clear linear trend is evident: children's scores on these tests are positively related to their SES.

Panel B of Figure 1.3 presents these differences, again, in effect-size units, with low-SES, low-middle-SES, high-middle, and high-SES groups each compared to middle-SES children (the third quintile, which we call "middle class"). Although a general linear trend is still evident, two addi-

FIGURE 1.3   Math and reading achievement at the beginning of kindergarten

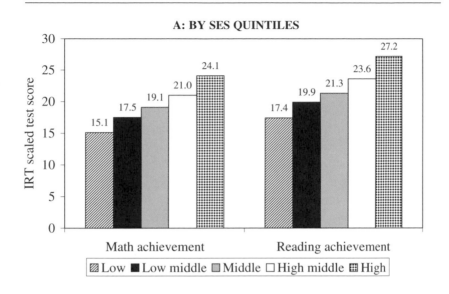

A: BY SES QUINTILES

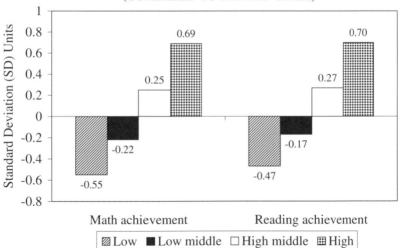

B: UNADJUSTED SES DIFFERENCES, EFFECT SIZES
(COMPARED TO MIDDLE CLASS)

Source: Authors' analysis of U.S. Department of Education ECLS-K data.

tional findings emerge when results are presented this way. First, young children's SES and cognitive status are strongly related, that is, SES differences in achievement status at kindergarten entry are very large. Recall that comparisons here are with middle-SES children, not between high- and low-SES children (where effect-size comparisons would be considerably larger). Low-SES children score .55 SD below middle-SES children in mathematics, and .47 SD below the same group in reading. Even more striking, high-SES children outscore their middle-SES counterparts by .69 SD in mathematics and .70 SD in reading. Second, the effect sizes of low-SES compared to lower-middle SES children on both achievement tests are more than twice as large, which is also the case in comparing high-middle and high-SES children to their middle-SES counterparts. Logically, effect sizes in test scores by SES are larger for the extreme quintiles than for the middle categories, in comparing them to middle-SES children.

Race differences by socioeconomic status. It is a well-known social phenomenon that race/ethnicity and SES are intertwined in the United States. That is, the families of children whose race/ethnicity is black or Hispanic are, in general, lower in terms of SES than are children from white families. **Figure 1.4** displays this relationship among the children in the ECLS-K sample, where we display the proportion of each racial/ethnic group in the SES quintiles. If race/ethnicity and SES were unrelated to one another, quintiles for each racial/ethnic group would contain exactly 20% of the sample. However, distributions by quintile are not at all equivalent for any racial/ethnic group. For example, only 9.3% of white children (the left-hand group in Figure 1.4) are in the low-SES group, whereas 33.8% of blacks, 28.5% of Hispanics, and 22.0% of others are in the low-SES category. It is clear that black and Hispanic children are substantially over-represented in the low-SES category, but white and Asian children are under-represented. Similarly, white (27.4%) and especially Asian children (39.5%) are over-represented in the high-SES category, whereas very few families of black (7.5%) and Hispanic children (9.8%) are in the high-SES quintile. This display makes it clear that the "other" race category more closely resembles black and Hispanic than white and Asian children, at least in terms of their family SES.

The especially damaging combination of race and class for children's achievement. We have seen large race differences in entering achievement regardless of social class (Figure 1.2), large SES differences in entering achievement regardless of race (Figure 1.3), and the strong relationship

FIGURE 1.4   Kindergartner's family social class distribution (quintiles) by Race

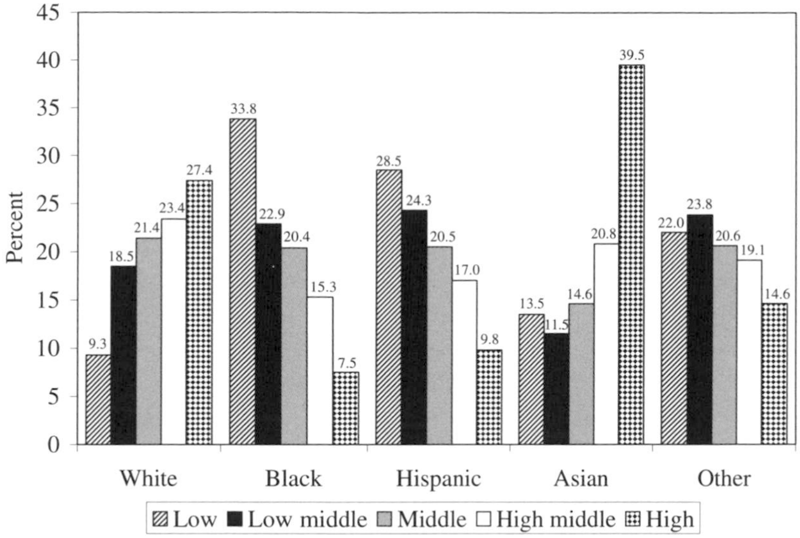

Source: Authors' analysis of U.S. Department of Education ECLS-K data.

between race and SES (Figure 1.4). If we take both into consideration at the same time, achievement differences are very large. **Figure 1.5** compares the achievement of disadvantaged blacks and Hispanics (children in the first SES quintile, which includes a third of all black children and more than a quarter of all Hispanic children) to middle class whites (children in the third SES quintile) and to advantaged whites (children in the fifth SES quintile). In order to facilitate comparisons in this figure, we re-scaled the tests to standard deviation (or effect-size) units, by converting the original IRT scores to z-scores (mean=0, SD=1).

Disadvantaged black children enter kindergarten more than half a standard deviation below the national average (.68 SD *below* the mean in math, .56 SD *below* the mean in reading). Low-SES Hispanic children enter at a similar disadvantage (.71 SD *below* the mean in math, .69 SD *below* the mean in reading). On the other hand, middle class white children score at or near the national average (.06 SD *above* the mean in math, .03 SD *below* the mean in reading), and advantaged white children score far above the national average (.70 SD *above* the mean in math, .64 SD *above* the mean in reading). Looked at from this perspective, the overall

FIGURE 1.5 Math and reading achievement at the beginning of kindergarten: Comparing disadvantaged black and Hispanic children to middle class and advantaged white children

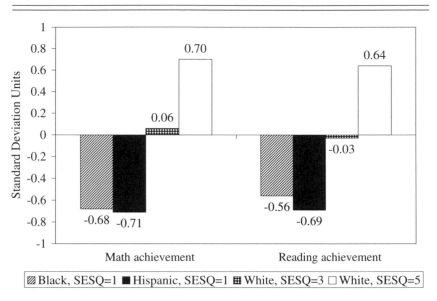

Source: Authors' analysis of U.S. Department of Education ECLS-K data.

black/white and hispanic/white gaps in Figure 1.2 underestimate much of the disparity, mainly because SES and race/ethnicity are so closely intertwined. Entering achievement differences between low-SES black children and middle class white children are around .7 SD in math and .6 SD in reading. Entering achievement differences between low-SES black children and high-SES white children are around 1.4 SD in math and 1.2 SD in reading.

Summary

The results from this chapter suggest that children present themselves at the schoolhouse door for the first time with considerable variation in cognitive status. Of great social import but yet unsurprising, there are substantial differences in children's performance on cognitive tests of mathematics and reading administered at the beginning of the kindergarten year by race, ethnicity, and SES. Children who are black, Hispanic, or members of the "other" racial group score considerably below white children as they

begin school, whereas Asian children score somewhat above their white counterparts. There are also large differences in children's cognitive performance as they begin school in terms of social class, with higher-SES children scoring higher and lower-SES children lower on achievement tests in both reading and mathematics. An important finding from this chapter is that disparities in children's cognitive status at school entry by SES are actually larger than those by race/ethnicity. Thus, even at "the starting gate"—when all U.S. children enroll in school for the first time—certain children (particularly those who are black, Hispanic, or lower SES) enter school both cognitively and socially disadvantaged. Thus, inequality by social background at the educational starting gate is substantial, and even more substantial given the combined impact of having a low SES *and* being black or Hispanic.

Although this picture of inequality is in one sense very clear—children with social disadvantage also enter school with a cognitive disadvantage, there may be more to this picture. Other features of children's home lives are likely to be associated with both their social background and their cognitive status. We pursue these issues in the next two chapters.

**TABLE 2.1   ECLS-K starting gate: descriptives by race
(n=16,157 children)** *(cont.)*

	White	Black	Hispanic	Asian	Other
At-home activities:					
Hours TV weekly, mean	13.2	17.9	15.1	13.4	15.2
(SD)	(7.1)	(9.8)	(8.9)	(8.6)	(9.0)
Watching Sesame Street	53.7	80.3	69.2	70.1	65.8
Number of books, mean	93.1	39.6	52.5	55.8	62.6
(SD)	(59.1)	(39.9)	(48.7)	(53.3)	(55.3)
Number of records/					
tapes/CDs, mean	17.6	10.6	12.2	17.0	13.1
(SD)	(18.4)	(14.5)	(17.2)	(18.7)	(16.5)
Own home computer	65.7	32.9	41.5	64.8	45.0
Frequency of play activities					
(% who report 3-6 times a week or everyday)					
Parent & child play games	63.6%	59.8%	58.3%	58.2%	63.7%
Parent & child build things	40.0	37.1	37.0	36.1	39.8
Child does sports	57.0	55.4	50.8	43.5	56.1
Parent teaches child about nature	34.9	24.9	27.2	24.0	34.7
Parent helps child make art	55.6	50.3	48.3	56.4	56.2
Parent tells child stories	57.7	50.5	54.4	56.6	61.2
Parent & child sing songs	72.8	75.1	69.8	56.9	71.2
Child does chores	81.8	78.4	73.9	66.2	79.4
Play composite					
Z-score, mean	0.04	-0.03	-0.14	0.22	0.09
(SD)	(0.95)	(1.06)	(1.04)	(1.01)	(1.01)
Frequency of Reading Activities					
(% who report 3-6 times a week or everyday)					
Child reads books					
outside of school	68.7%	73.8%	66.4%	71.8%	70.2%
Child reads picture books	85.9	75.1	75.3	75.7	81.1
Parent reads to child	86.6	67.5	74.8	77.8	78.0
Reading composite					
Z-score, mean	0.07	-0.13	-0.14	0.00	-0.04
(SD)	(0.95)	(1.03)	(1.01)	(1.01)	(1.02)
Outside-home (non-school) activities:					
Visit zoo/aquarium	39.4%	43.5%	44.9%	44.2%	33.8%
Visit museum	33.0	28.0	28.0	38.1	28.5
Visit library	56.0	48.8	48.5	67.8	46.3
Attend play/concert/show	39.9	38.3	36.4	41.2	34.4
Participate in athletic events	57.9	25.8	32.9	31.0	38.1
Attend sporting event	47.4	38.5	41.5	26.7	41.6
Participate in organized clubs	16.6	10.2	9.8	7.2	11.1
Participate in					
organized performing	15.5	20.4	8.7	8.3	10.7
Take dance lessons	20.2	10.0	13.8	16.3	14.3
Take music lessons	7.7	7.0	5.8	18.4	8.7
Take drama classes	1.9	1.4	1.2	1.9	1.3
Take art lessons	8.3	5.9	5.4	10.3	9.0
Take craft classes	13.3	7.3	8.5	8.8	11.1

Source: Authors' analysis of U.S. Department of Education ECLS-K data.

**TABLE 2.1   ECLS-K starting gate: descriptives by race
(n=16,157 children)**

	White	Black	Hispanic	Asian	Other
Unweighted sample size	9786	2536	2143	761	931
Weighted percentages	61.7	17.3	13.9	2.3	4.8
Entering achievement:					
Fall math achievement, mean	21.0	16.5	17.1	22.2	17.4
(SD)	(7.4)	(5.4)	(6.2)	(8.4)	(6.7)
Fall reading achievement, mean	23.2	19.9	19.5	25.7	19.9
(SD)	(8.5)	(6.9)	(7.4)	(10.9)	(8.2)
Social background and child demographics:					
SES, mean	0.22	-0.51	-0.36	0.48	-0.22
(SD)	(0.95)	(0.96)	(0.88)	(1.13)	(1.02)
Age in months, mean	66.4	65.9	65.7	65.2	65.9
(SD)	(4.4)	(4.4)	(4.3)	(4.1)	(4.6)
Female	48.3%	48.8%	49.0%	50.1%	48.2%
Non-English households	1.3%	0.9%	30.7%	50.5%	4.8%
Kindergarten repeaters	4.2%	5.4%	5.2%	3.5%	4.7%
Home demographics:					
Single parent households	15.0%	53.7%	26.9%	9.6%	29.2%
With no younger siblings	56.0	55.3	56.7	60.2	53.2
With 1 younger sibling	35.6	30.9	34.1	33.1	24.7
With 2 or more younger siblings	8.4	13.8	9.2	6.7	12.1
With no older siblings	42.1	35.9	40.5	44.6	41.8
With 1 older sibling	38.4	34.2	35.1	36.2	29.0
With 2 older siblings	15.0	18.5	16.8	13.6	16.0
With 3 or more older siblings	4.5	11.4	7.6	5.6	13.2
With no siblings	15.4	17.9	18.6	20.6	19.5
Lived in one home since birth	37.5	31.7	28.5	36.3	30.9
Lived in two homes since birth	32.1	35.8	36.3	36.5	34.8
Lived in three homes since birth	16.8	20.1	19.8	17.3	19.5
Lived in four homes since birth	7.4	7.5	9.0	7.4	7.8
Lived in five/more homes since birth	6.2%	45.9%	6.4%	2.6%	7.0%
Live in large city	8.2	29.2	29.2	28.0	12.6
Live in medium city	18.7	26.6	22.5	17.5	17.5
Live in suburban/urban fringe	46.8	33.0	37.6	44.8	27.5
Live in rural/small town	26.3	11.2	10.7	9.6	42.4
Educational expectations and primary pre-kindergarten day care:					
HS graduation or less	9.7%	13.0%	9.6%	1.8%	12.7%
Some college or college degree	68.8	53.9	53.2	50.6	60.0
Masters, MD, or Ph.D.	21.4	33.1	37.2	47.6	27.4
Center-based care	49.1	33.4	33.7	46.8	30.5
Head Start	5.5	22.8	13.4	6.6	18.7
Parental care only	16.9	12.9	21.8	19.8	18.8
Non-parental, relative care	11.2	18.4	18.0	18.6	18.7
Non-relative care	12.7	4.4	8.0	5.2	7.5
Primary care varied	4.6	8.1	5.1	3.1	6.0

(cont.)

3.   *Expectations for them and their educational experiences* (e.g., what level of education their parents expect for them; the care or preschool experiences they had in the previous year—child care, Head Start, with relatives, in a child-care center, or at home with a parent);

4.   *Activities in their homes* (e.g., time spent watching television; the number of books or other media in the home; whether the family has a computer at home; the frequency of play activities; the frequency of reading activities); and

5.   *Activities outside their homes* (e.g., cultural visits, such as museums, a zoo, the library, or shows; participation in athletics or clubs; lessons, such as dance, music, drama, and arts and crafts).

The information about family demographics and activities in these five categories came from parents' reports in the ECLS-K surveys, most of which were collected at the beginning of the kindergarten year.[8] Descriptive differences by racial/ethnic status and social class across this wide array of family demographics and home activities are shown in **Tables 2.1** and **2.2**. The results in Table 2.1 display subgroup means for each of the demographics and activities we consider separately for the five racial/ethnic groups; Table 2.2 results display subgroup means on the same demographics and activities for the SES quintiles.

Social background and demographic characteristics

Language status and kindergarten repetition. Of the many children's demographic characteristics we investigated, we highlight two: whether or not the child lives in a non-English speaking household (defined in terms of the principal language used in the home), and whether the child is repeating kindergarten. The proportions of ECLS-tested children who live in households where the *main language* spoken is other than English are displayed in **Figure 2.1**. Unsurprisingly, panel A, which displays racial/ethnic differences, shows that very few white or black children's parents speak languages other than English at home, whereas almost a third of Hispanic children's home language is not English (30.7%). In about half of the Asian children's homes English is the major language spoken. Only a small proportion of children in the "other" racial group (4.8%) live in non-English-speaking households. We suspect that these are mostly Native Americans.[9]

The trend by SES (panel B of Figure 2.1) is more striking: a higher percentage of children from low-SES backgrounds live in non-English

CHAPTER 2

Young children's social disadvantage and family activities

This chapter explores how children's social background, particularly race/ethnicity and SES, is associated with other features of their home lives. Chapter 1 examined how social background can substantially affect children's cognitive status as they start school. Black and Hispanic children, as well as children in the "other" racial/ethnic category, score considerably below their white and Asian counterparts on tests of academic achievement in math and reading at kindergarten entry. Moreover, family SES is also associated strongly with children's cognitive status. Our analyses here—which are also descriptive—are motivated by a large body of research that demonstrates that beyond race and social class differences, children's academic achievement is also influenced by many other features of their homes and families. In this chapter we consider how a wide range of family activities differ according to children's race, ethnicity, and SES.

Home demographics and family activities

Numerous studies have shown that a wide range of family demographic characteristics, attitudes, and activities, beyond race/ethnicity and socio-economic status, are associated with children's cognitive performance. This chapter considers a large number of such factors that typify children's homes and families at the point they enter kindergarten. These factors can be arranged into five categories:

1. *Children's demographic background* (e.g., age, gender, whether they come from non-English speaking homes, whether they are repeating kindergarten);

2. *The demographics of their homes* (e.g., whether the household is headed by a single parent; the numbers of older and younger siblings; family residential mobility; the types of communities in which their homes are located);

TABLE 2.2   ECLS-K starting gate: descriptives by SES quintiles

	Low	Low middle	Middle	High middle	High
At-home activities:					
Hours TV weekly, mean	13.2	17.9	15.1	13.4	15.2
Unweighted sample size	2434	3115	3336	3516	3756
Weighted percentages	16.9	20.2	20.9	20.8	21.2
Entering Achievement:					
Fall math achievement, mean	15.1	17.5	19.1	21.0	24.1
(SD)	(5.1)	(5.9)	(6.3)	(6.8)	(8.1)
Fall reading achievement, mean	17.4	20.0	21.3	23.6	27.2
(SD)	(5.4)	(6.6)	(7.2)	(8.2)	(9.9)
Social background and child demographics:					
White	34.0%	56.6%	63.2%	69.3%	79.8%
Black	34.5	19.6	16.8	12.7	6.1
Hispanic	23.4	16.8	13.7	11.4	6.4
Asian	1.8	1.3	1.6	2.3	4.3
Other	6.3	5.7	4.7	4.4	3.3
Female	47.1	48.7	49.4	48.7	49.0
Non-English households	14.0	7.1	4.3	4.8	4.5
Kindergarten repeaters	8.1	4.7	4.4	3.2	3.1
Age in months, mean	66.5	66.2	66.1	66.1	66.0
(SD)	(4.7)	(4.4)	(4.3)	(4.2)	(4.3)
Home demographics:					
Single parent households	48.2%	29.3%	22.4%	14.7%	10.2%
With no younger siblings	49.9	57.0	58.6	58.4	54.2
With 1 younger sibling	34.2	33.6	33.5	34.6	36.8
With 2 or more younger siblings	15.9	9.4	7.9	7.0	9.0
With no older siblings	35.6	39.6	41.8	43.1	43.0
With 1 older sibling	33.5	35.9	36.4	39.2	38.0
With 2 older siblings	19.3	16.3	16.1	12.9	15.3
With 3/more older siblings	11.6	8.2	5.7	4.8	3.7
With no siblings	14.7	17.8	18.3	18.0	13.6
Lived in one home since birth	28.0	30.6	34.1	38.5	41.6
Lived in two homes since birth	32.4	31.9	33.4	34.1	35.5
Lived in three homes since birth	19.3	22.6	21.6	19.8	16.7
Lived in four homes since birth	20.0	24.2	21.4	17.5	16.9
Lived in five/more homes since birth	8.5	7.9	6.6	7.4	3.1
Live in large city	19.9	15.2	14.9	13.6	13.9
Live in medium city	23.2	20.5	20.5	19.8	19.8
Live in suburban/urban fringe	28.6	37.5	40.0	48.3	52.8
Live in rural/small town	28.3	26.7	24.6	18.1	13.5
Educational expectations and primary pre-kindergarten day care:					
HS graduation or less	28.1%	15.6%	7.8%	3.3%	1.1%
Some college or college degree	50.1	61.8	69.1	71.1	61.6
Masters, MD, or Ph.D.	21.7	22.6	23.2	25.7	37.3
Center-based care	20.1	31.2	41.7	52.2	65.0
Head Start	27.0	14.6	8.6	3.9	1.1
Parental care only	25.9	21.3	16.5	14.9	9.4
Non-parental, relative care	16.8	18.9	16.4	11.5	6.7
Non-relative care	4.7	8.3	11.1	11.9	13.9
Primary care varied	5.4	5.7	5.8	5.7	3.9

(cont.)

TABLE 2.2   ECLS-K starting gate: descriptives by SES quintiles *(cont.)*

	Low	Low middle	Middle	High middle	High
At-home activities:					
Hours TV weekly, mean	17.2	15.9	14.5	13.3	11.6
(SD)	(10.0)	(8.6)	(7.9)	(6.8)	(6.3)
Watching Sesame Street	72.8%	63.8%	61.3%	59.8%	51.7%
Number of books, mean	38.0	60.4	76.0	88.6	108.1
(SD)	(41.2)	(50.8)	(55.6)	(58.5)	(60.3)
Number of records/					
tapes/CDs, mean	8.1	12.5	15.3	17.6	21.8
(SD)	(13.8)	(16.5)	(17.5)	(17.8)	(19.4)
Own home computer	19.9%	38.3%	54.7%	71.5%	84.7%
Frequency of play activities					
(% who report 3-6 times a week or everyday)					
Parent & child play games	56.1%	60.3%	60.3%	65.1%	67.3%
Parent & child build things	38.3	38.4	37.8	39.5	40.7
Child does sports	53.6	54.4	54.9	56.9	57.5
Parent teaches child about nature	24.1	27.9	31.5	33.9	40.0
Parent helps child make art	46.3	51.3	53.3	56.5	59.4
Parent tells child stories	46.7	54.5	54.8	59.0	63.8
Parent & child sing songs	67.0	70.4	72.6	74.8	75.8
Child does chores	73.5	78.7	81.0	81.4	82.3
Play composite Z-score, mean	-0.16	-0.06	-0.01	0.05	0.15
(SD)	(1.13)	(1.02)	(0.98)	(0.93)	(0.89)
Frequency of reading activities					
(% who report 3-6 times a week or everyday)					
Child reads books					
outside of school	65.1%	68.1%	69.3%	70.2%	73.0%
Child reads picture books	69.6	79.1	83.7	85.6	89.8
Parent reads to child	62.6	76.6	80.7	87.3	93.9
Reading composite					
Z-score, mean	-0.29	-0.11	-0.04	0.07	0.28
(SD)	(1.12)	(1.00)	(0.97)	(0.95)	(0.87)
Outside-home (non-school) activities:					
Visit zoo/aquarium	35.4%	39.0%	39.8%	43.0%	44.7%
Visit museum	20.2	24.7	28.3	34.7	45.6
Visit library	35.7	46.7	53.3	60.2	66.9
Attend play/concert/show	27.1	33.9	38.9	43.0	48.4
Participate in athletic events	20.1%	33.2%	45.7%	57.6%	72.6%
Attend sporting event	29.7	38.4	46.1	49.0	54.6
Participate in organized clubs	7.5	9.5	13.7	17.5	20.5
Participate in					
organized performing	8.7%	10.3%	13.7%	17.0%	23.3%
Take dance lessons	5.8	9.8	14.7	21.7	30.8
Take music lessons	2.6	3.6	5.5	8.0	16.6
Take drama classes	0.7	0.4	1.2	1.9	3.8
Take art lessons	3.9%	4.5%	5.9%	8.3%	14.0%
Take craft classes	5.4	7.4	10.6	13.0	18.8

Source: Authors' analysis of U.S. Department of Education ECLS-K data.

FIGURE 2.1   Percent of kindergartners in non-English speaking households

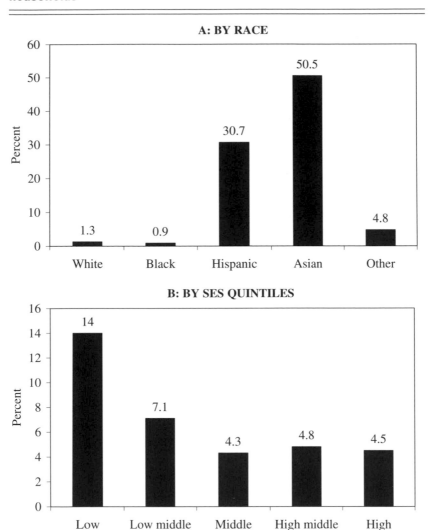

A: BY RACE

Source: Authors' analysis of U.S. Department of Education ECLS-K data.

households (14%) than children from middle-SES to high-SES homes (under 5%). The families of children living in non-English households are mostly low SES, and they are quite likely Hispanic or Asian. The proportions of children repeating kindergarten is quite small (less than 5%—**Figure 2.2**).[10] The proportions are quite similar across the racial/ethnic

FIGURE 2.2   Percent of kindergartners who are repeating kindergarten

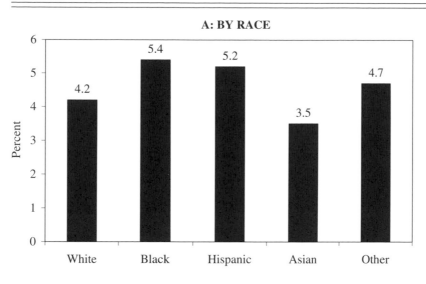

A: BY RACE

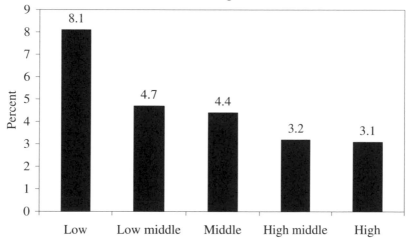

B: BY SES QUINTILES

Source: Authors' analysis of U.S. Department of Education ECLS-K data.

groups (see panel A), with kindergarten repetition only slightly more likely for black and Hispanic children (5.4% and 5.2%, respectively) than for whites (4.2%). Considerably more striking is the trend between repeating kindergarten and SES (panel B of Figure 2.2). Low-SES children are almost twice as likely as the four other SES categories to repeat kindergarten.

FIGURE 2.3   Percent of kindergartners from single-parent homes

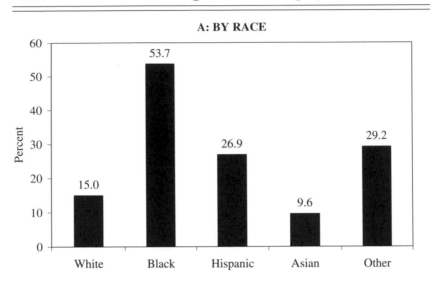

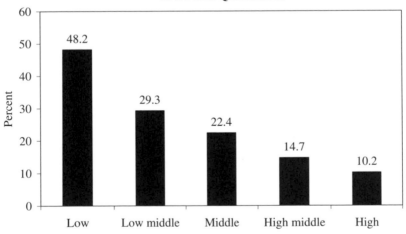

Source: Authors' analysis of U.S. Department of Education ECLS-K data.

Single parents, family size, and residence. We give special focus to three of the 18 home demographic characteristics presented in Tables 2.1 and 2.2 that we consider especially important: single-parent households, family size, and residential location.

As shown in **Figure 2.3**, the proportion of young children living in single-parent households, a major indicator of family structure, is much

higher for socially disadvantaged children. Panel A shows that over half of black kindergartners in 1998 lived in single-parent households (53.7%), compared to slightly more than a fourth of Hispanic (26.9%) and "other" children (29.3%). Single-parent households are much less common for white (15%) and Asian children (9.6%). As striking as the racial differences in family structure are, so too are differences by SES (panel B of Figure 2.3). The relationship between SES and single-parent family structure is strong and close to linear—that is, as SES goes up, the proportion of young children in single-parent homes goes down. Almost half the kindergartners in the lowest SES quintile live in single-parent homes. Certainly, the causal order here is unknown.[11]

The theory of resource diminution would suggest that parents' ability to provide their young children with time and attention is diminished by their need to care for other children in the household. We measured the *number* of siblings each child had in several ways, as well as whether the siblings were *older* or *younger* than the child. **Figure 2.4** presents the proportion of America's kindergartners with *two or more younger siblings*, separately for race and SES. In **Figure 2.5** we present the same categories for the proportions of children with *three or more older siblings*. For both types of large families (i.e., with younger and older siblings), the proportions for black and "other" racial groups are higher than for whites, Hispanics, and especially Asians (whose family sizes are lowest, shown in panel A of Figures 2.4 and 2.5). For example, 13.8% of young black children have at least two younger siblings, and 11.4% have at least three older siblings. This compares to 8.4% and 4.6% for younger and older siblings, respectively, for white children.

There is a clear pattern for family size by SES (panel B of Figures 2.4 and 2.5): less-advantaged children have more siblings. Higher proportions of children in the lowest SES quintile (15.9%) have many younger siblings, and 11.6% have many older siblings. As children's family SES increases, the proportion of children with three or more older siblings declines; only 3.7% of high-SES children have many older siblings. The trend is less linear for many younger siblings, where the high-middle SES group has the lowest proportion (7.0%). Clearly, large family size is associated with race and SES, with black children and low-SES children most likely to have many siblings either older or younger than themselves.

The types of communities in which children reside (city size, suburban or rural location) are also associated with their social background. Results in panel A of **Figure 2.6** indicate that, although almost half of white (46.8%) and Asian (44.8%) children reside in suburban communities, only about a third of black (33%) and Hispanic (37.6%) children live

FIGURE 2.4 Percent of kindergartners with two or more younger siblings

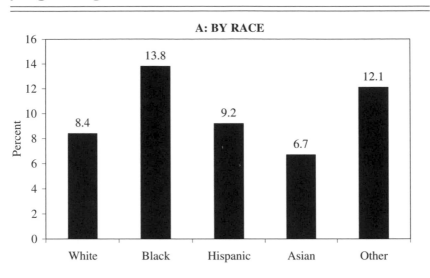

A: BY RACE

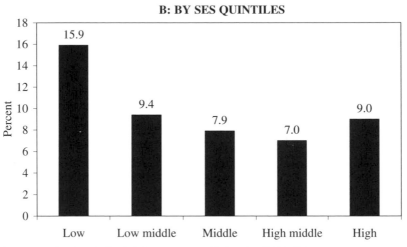

B: BY SES QUINTILES

Source: Authors' analysis of U.S. Department of Education ECLS-K data.

in the suburbs. Close to 30% of black, Hispanic, and Asian children live in large cities, which is more than triple the proportion of white children (8.2%). More than twice the proportion of white children live in rural areas or small towns (26.3%), compared to about 10% of blacks, Hispanics, and Asians. Almost half the children in the "other" racial group (42.4%) reside in rural areas (mostly likely to be Native Americans). In terms of

FIGURE 2.5   Percent of kindergartners with three or more older siblings

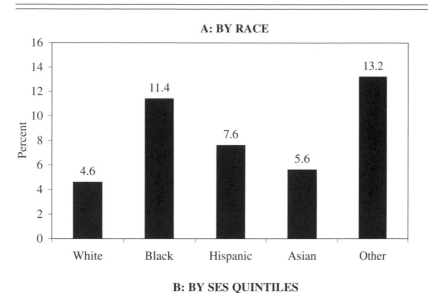

A: BY RACE

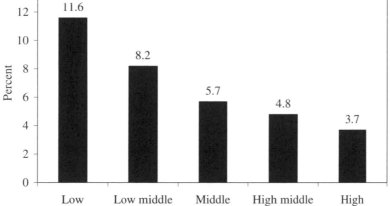

B: BY SES QUINTILES

Source: Authors' analysis of U.S. Department of Education ECLS-K data.

residential location, Asian children more closely resemble other minorities than whites, as few live in rural areas and many in cities.

There are three clear residential location patterns by SES (panel B of Figure 2.6). As SES goes up, the proportion of children living in the suburbs also goes up. Correspondingly, as SES goes up, the proportion of children living in either larger cities or rural areas goes down. Almost double

FIGURE 2.6   Percent of kindergartners who live in large cities, medium cities, suburban/urban fringe, or rural/small towns

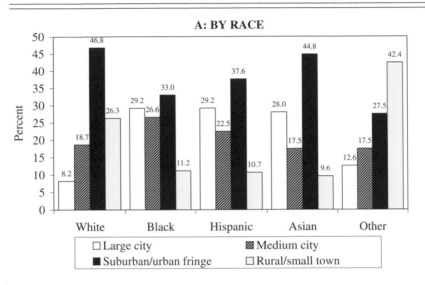

A: BY RACE

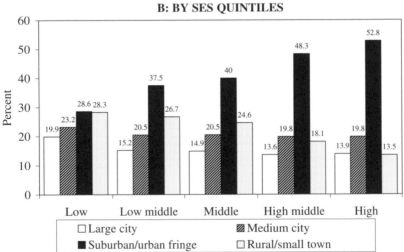

B: BY SES QUINTILES

Source: Authors' analysis of U.S. Department of Education ECLS-K data.

the proportion of high- as low-SES children live in suburban areas (52.8% vs. 28.6%), but comparisons among SES groups for other residential locations are less stark. Around 20% of children live in medium-sized cities, regardless of socioeconomic status.

Social background and child care experiences. Although it is possible that children's experiences the year before kindergarten influence their subsequent academic performance, unfortunately we are unable to distinguish between experiences in child care (which may have no academic component) and/or preschool (which may have an academic component) with these ECLS-K data. We present information on two child care conditions here: center-based care (which may be akin to preschool—**Figure 2.7**) and Head Start, which is a federally funded preschool restricted to low-income children (**Figure 2.8**).[12] White and Asian children are most likely to have experienced center-based care (almost half of all children in those racial groups), whereas about one third of children in other racial/ethnic groups attended center-based care the year prior to kindergarten (panel A).

The proportional representation of children by SES in center-based care (panel B) is more revealing. As children's SES goes up, so does the proportion of them with center-based care experience. The proportion of high-SES children with center-based care is over three times as large as low-SES children (65.0% vs. 20.1%). The comparison between center-based care and Head Start experience (Figure 2.8) shows one to be almost a mirror image of the other. Many blacks and "other" racial group children are likely to have experienced Head Start (panel A, 22.8% and 18.7%, respectively), whereas much lower proportions of whites and Asians had this experience (5.5% and 6.6%). Hispanic children's experience with Head Start falls midway between whites' and blacks.' Understandably (because of eligibility requirements), a much greater proportion of poor children are served by Head Start programs than higher-SES children (panel B). The small percentages of middle-class and more affluent children who are served by Head Start may be because the program is also mandated to enroll handicapped children of preschool age.

Social background and family activities. Among the large number of at-home activities shown in Tables 2.1 and 2.2, we focus on five that have been shown to have special relevance to learning: parents' reports of the amount of time their children spend watching television, the number of children's books in the home, the time parents report reading to their children, whether there is a computer in the home, and use of the library.

The number of hours per week that young children's parents report that they watch television (reported in the spring of the kindergarten year) is displayed in **Figure 2.9** (also see endnote 8). Although there are racial/ethnic differences, they are not large (e.g., black children spend 17.9 hours/week watching TV, compared to 13.2 hours for whites). However, the trend for SES, although not as strong as other home activities considered

FIGURE 2.7   Percent of kindergartners who attended center-based preschool

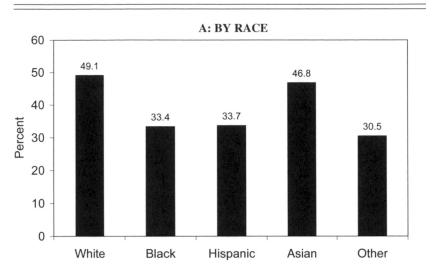

A: BY RACE

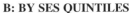

B: BY SES QUINTILES

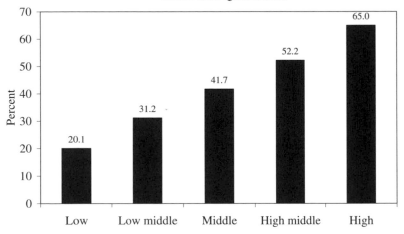

Source: Authors' analysis of U.S. Department of Education ECLS-K data.

in this report, is linear. That is, as SES goes up, the hours children watch TV goes down. The difference between even the extreme SES groups (high- vs. low-SES) is, however, less than 5 hours/week. Regardless of SES, race, or ethnicity, kindergarten-aged children spend an average of two hours every day in front of their families' television sets.

FIGURE 2.8   Percent of kindergartners who attended Head Start

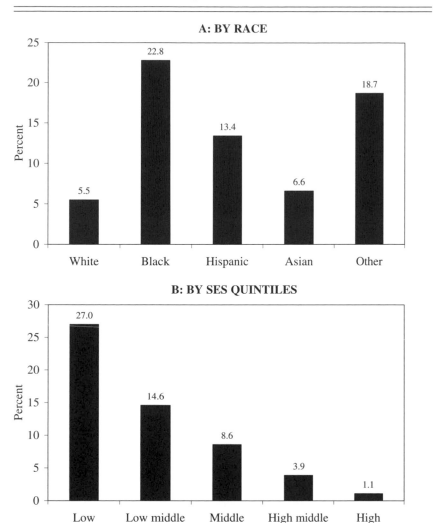

A: BY RACE

B: BY SES QUINTILES

Source: Authors' analysis of U.S. Department of Education ECLS-K data.

We considered several family activities that are related to literacy in Tables 2.1 and 2.2. **Figure 2.10** displays race/ethnicity and SES differences in the numbers of children's books parents report owning. On average, white children own over twice as many books as black children (93 vs. 40 books), with Hispanic and Asian children quite similar (about 50 books—panel A). There is a clear trend of children's book ownership by

FIGURE 2.9   Kindergartners' weekly TV watching

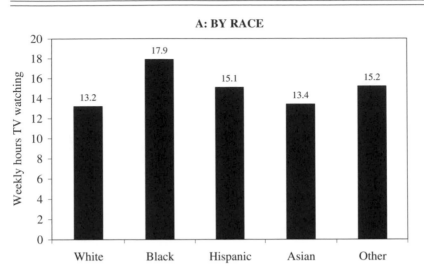

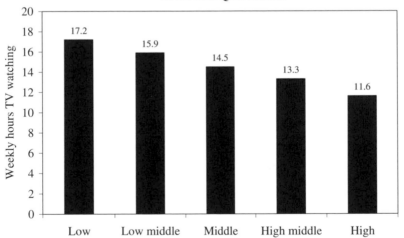

Source: Authors' analysis of U.S. Department of Education ECLS-K data.

SES, not surprising given that families must buy these books. High-SES children own about three times as many books as low-SES children, with the SES categories forming a linear trend. Of course, parents could read to their children from books borrowed from the library as well as books they own.

FIGURE 2.10   Number of books kindergartner owns

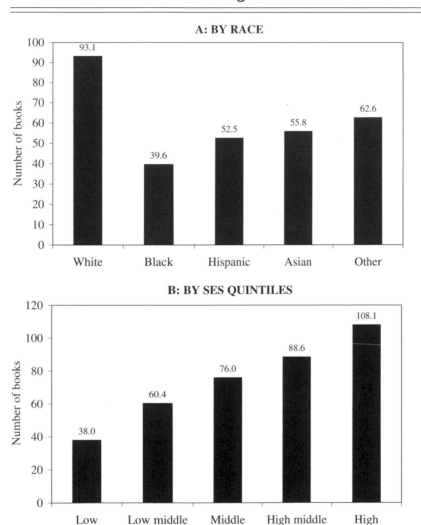

A: BY RACE

B: BY SES QUINTILES

Source: Authors' analysis of U.S. Department of Education ECLS-K data.

A costly household item that may influence learning—a computer—shows clear relationships with race/ethnicity and SES (**Figure 2.11**). About two-thirds of white and Asian children's homes contain a computer, which is about twice the proportion of black children with computers in their homes (32.9%). Given the high cost of a home computer, it is not surprising that family SES is strongly related to computer ownership. Almost all

FIGURE 2.11 Percent of kindergartners with a computer in the home

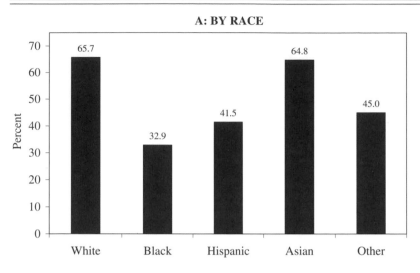

A: BY RACE

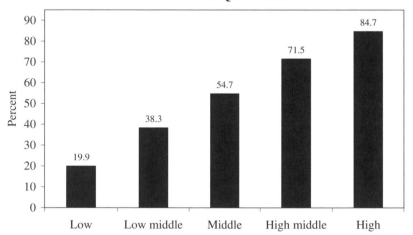

B: BY SES QUINTILES

Source: Authors' analysis of U.S. Department of Education ECLS-K data.

high-SES children's homes have a computer (84.7%), over four times the proportion as low-SES homes with computers (19.9%). Although computer ownership may also be linked with parents' familiarity with computers from the workplace and children's book buying associated with parents' own reading habits and skills, these findings also represent important choices about resource allocation—book and especially computer owner-

ship are strongly associated with both race/ethnicity and SES. No such relationship is evident concerning a television set—virtually all U.S. families own TVs, and indeed many have multiple sets. Nonetheless, computer ownership is no longer a rare event, even for relatively low-SES families.

Most parents indicate that they read to their children between 3 and 6 times per week (or more), as shown in **Figure 2.12** (as reported at the beginning of the kindergarten year). However, these high proportions vary by race (panel A) and SES (panel B). Considerably higher proportions of white children's parents report reading often to their children compared to black children's parents (86.6% vs. 67.5%), with the proportions for Hispanic and Asian children's parents in between. The link between reading often to children and SES is also linear, with more high-SES than low-SES parents reporting reading to their children 3-6 times a week (93.9% as compared to 62.6%). Of course, this could be explained by lack of books or lack of reading skill among low-SES parents, especially those with weak English language skills. Beyond the information about the frequency of reading, we have no information about the duration or content of the reading.

An outside-the-home family activity, visiting the public library, is part of parents' literacy activity with their children (see **Figure 2.13**). Although owning books costs money, borrowing books from the public library is usually free. Access to libraries is probably more common in urban and suburban areas than in rural areas, and this also varies among urban and suburban areas of different resource bases. Moreover, access to (and the cost of) transportation is a resource-based issue for library use. These considerations surely help to explain the linear relationship between library use during the kindergarten year and SES (panel B); as SES goes up, so does the probability of children visiting the library with a parent. However, racial patterns are somewhat different than we have observed for other family activities. Asian parents report visiting the library with their children more often than white parents (67.8% vs. 56%); about half of Hispanic and black parents report visiting the library with their children. There is no information in ECLS-K about the frequency or duration of library visits.

Summary

Among the broad set of child and family demographics and activities considered in this chapter, we chose a few to discuss and display graphically. Patterns by social background are quite consistent. Demographic factors that are generally seen as rendering children at risk of school failure—such as single-parent family structure, lack of English usage in the house-

FIGURE 2.12   Percent of kindergartners whose parents read to them three to six times per week or everyday

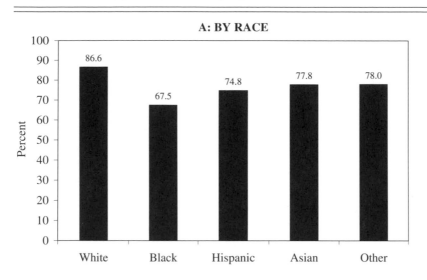

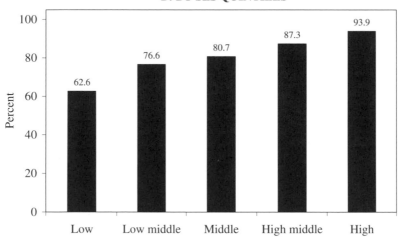

Source: Authors' analysis of U.S. Department of Education ECLS-K data.

hold, large family size, residing in a large city or a rural area—are more common among black and Hispanic children and their families; the frequencies of these risk factors are also negatively related to family socioeconomic status. On the other hand, factors generally seen as advantageous for children's school progress—suburban residence, center-based

FIGURE 2.13   Percent of kindergartners who visit the public library

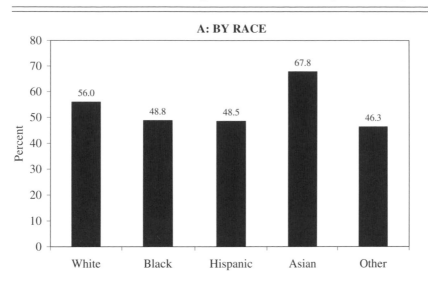

A: BY RACE

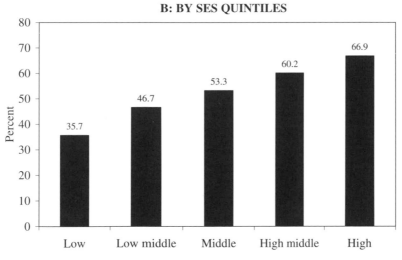

B: BY SES QUINTILES

Source: TK

child care experience, owning children's books, being read to frequently, owning an in-home computer, and visiting the public library—are more common among white and Asian children and those from higher-SES families. That Head Start enrollees are mostly low-SES children suggests that the program has been successful in enrolling its target population.

In Chapter 1 we learned that kindergarten children's social background is associated with their cognitive status. The presentation and discussion of results in this chapter indicate that families' activities and demographic characteristics are also socially differentiated. However, we still do not know whether (and how) these factors are associated with children's cognitive performance. We investigate two issues relevant to this question in the next chapter: (1) how this large array of family activities and demographics is associated with achievement, and (2) whether including them in a multivariate analysis reduces the magnitude of the links between children's race, ethnicity, SES, and their cognitive performance as they begin kindergarten.

CHAPTER 3

Understanding how social disadvantage relates to academic status

The aim of this chapter is to explore whether the magnitude of the association between the effect of children's social background (in particular their race/ethnicity and SES) and their achievement scores in mathematics and reading at the beginning of kindergarten is diminished once we take into account the various features of family demographics and activities (see Chapter 2). One purpose here is to understand (in essence, to "explain away") the link between social background and achievement by statistically adjusting for these other family factors. Analyses described in Chapters 1 and 2 are *descriptive*, that is, they explored how race, ethnicity, and social class are associated with children's cognitive performance at the beginning of kindergarten (Chapter 1) and how their family demographics and home activities are associated with children's racial, ethnic, and socioeconomic status (SES) (Chapter 2). The analyses described in this chapter are *more complex*, in that we take account of those family demographics and behaviors in estimating how race, ethnicity, and SES are associated with young children's achievement. This richer picture requires more complex analyses, ones that include many different factors in the same analyses. However, the focus is still on how race, ethnicity, and SES are linked with achievement as children begin their formal schooling.

Analysis strategy

The analyses described in this chapter are multivariate, meaning that they examine the association between social background and cognitive status while taking account of many other factors. The analyses use the same two achievement tests as outcomes that were the focus of Chapter 1. We employ a common statistical technique, called ordinary least squares regression, within a hierarchically structured format. That means that we entered groups of independent variables in logical steps, based on the several types of family demographics and activities introduced in Chapter 2. The analyses include all of the variables shown in Tables 2.1 and 2.2, not just the

subset of variables that were displayed in that chapter's graphs and discussion.

In the seven-step hierarchical regression analyses for this chapter, analytic models are cumulative: each subsequent step includes all variables from the previous steps. In particular, the structure is as follows:

- Step 1 includes only *race/ethnicity*;

- Step 2 adds *SES*;

- Step 3 introduces *child demographics* (non-English household, gender, age);

- Step 4 includes *family demographics* (family structure, numbers of older and younger siblings, residential mobility and location, neighborhood conditions);

- Step 5 adds *educational background* (parental expectations, experiences with preschool or child care during the previous year);

- Step 6 adds *at-home activities* (computer, TV watching, reading and play activities); and

- Step 7 adds other *out-of-home activities* (lessons and clubs, educational trips).

Because the hierarchical regression model is cumulative, Step 7 represents the full model, in that it includes the entire set of independent variables.[13] Although we display all coefficients in tables that report the full results of these regression analyses, our focus remains on the links between race/ethnicity, SES, and children's cognitive status at kindergarten entry—the same test scores described in Chapter 1. For example, we focus on *how the estimate for the black/white achievement gap changes after statistically controlling for family demographics and activities.* Because the analyses in this chapter are somewhat complex, we discuss the results for mathematics and reading achievement separately. Again, we present results as effect sizes (i.e., in SD units), so that they may be compared across outcomes and independent variables measured in different metrics. Recall that coefficients of .5 SD or above are considered "large," those between .3 and .5 SD "moderate," .1-.3 SD "small," and below .1 SD "trivial. Although statistical significance levels are shown in Tables 3.1 and 3.2, our focus is on effect sizes.

Explaining social background effects on math achievement at kindergarten entry

Race effects alone. **Table 3.1** displays the multivariate models examining children's achievement in mathematics as they enter kindergarten; **Table 3.2** displays the results of the same analysis for reading. Our discussion here focuses mostly on how the regression coefficients associated with race and SES on achievement change at each step. In the analyses in Tables 3.1 and 3.2, the racial/ethnic group differences are how each group's coefficient compares to whites'. We explore the SES effects in the same quintiles shown in earlier chapters. As before, each quintile is separately compared to quintile 3, middle-SES children.[14]

Although the patterns of results are relatively similar in Tables 3.1 (mathematics) and 3.2 (reading), we discuss Table 3.1 results in somewhat more detail. Step 1 of Table 3.1 is identical to results shown graphically in panel B of Figure 1.2: black children beginning kindergarten score .62 SD, Hispanics .54 SD, and children in the other racial group .50 SD *below* their white counterparts in mathematics achievement, all large effect sizes. Asian children's advantage over whites is small (.18 SD).

Race and SES effects. In step 2 of Table 3.1, the regression coefficients for racial/ethnic groups in math achievement are estimated taking children's family SES into account, just as the regression coefficients for SES take children's race/ethnicity into account (i.e., both the race and SES coefficients are adjusted for each other). Notice that once children's SES is taken into account, effect sizes for race/ethnicity *decline by about 40%* (e.g., the black/white difference drops from -.62 to -.36 SD; the Hispanic/white difference drops from -.54 to -.32 SD). Thus, the fact that, on average, black and Hispanic children's families are of lower SES "explains away" a substantial proportion of the initially observed racial/ethnic achievement gaps.

However, even adjusted for race/ethnicity the coefficients for SES are still large, as shown in step 2 on Table 3.1. Compared to middle-SES children, low-SES children score .45 SD lower in mathematics achievement and high-SES children score .62 SD higher. However, these SES effect sizes are smaller than they would be all alone, because children's race/ethnicity is taken into account. Recall from panel B of Figure 1.2, these same comparisons were -.55 SD (low vs. middle SES) and .69 SD (high vs. middle SES). It is noteworthy that *the magnitude of SES coefficients have declined much less (only about 10-15%) when children's race/ethnicity is taken into account than the race/ethnicity achievement gaps*

TABLE 3.1 ECLS-K starting gate: Math achievement at beginning of kindergarten (n=16,157 children)

	1. Race	2. Social class	3. Child demographics	4. Home demographics	5. Ed. expect. & pre-K care	6. At-home activities	7. Outside-home activities
Black	-0.62***	-0.36***	-0.32***	-0.30***	-0.31***	-0.21***	-0.21***
Hispanic	-0.54***	-0.32***	-0.23***	-0.24***	-0.25***	-0.20***	-0.19***
Asian	0.18***	0.12*	0.22***	0.20***	0.19***	0.22***	0.25***
Other	-0.50***	-0.34***	-0.32***	-0.26***	-0.26***	-0.20***	-0.20***
Low SES		-0.45***	-0.47***	-0.40***	-0.31***	-0.22***	-0.21***
Low Middle SES		-0.20***	-0.21***	-0.18***	-0.14***	-0.10***	-0.08***
High Middle SES		0.23***	0.23***	0.20***	0.17***	0.13***	0.12***
High SES		0.62***	0.62***	0.59***	0.51***	0.42***	0.39***
Female			0.03	0.03*	0.02	-0.01	-0.03*
Age			0.25***	0.26***	0.26***	0.26***	0.26***
Non-English Home			-0.10***	-0.13***	-0.17***	-0.11***	-0.09**
K-Repeater			-0.19***	-0.20***	-0.17***	-0.16***	-0.16***
Fall Test Time			0.08***	0.08***	0.07***	0.07***	0.07***
Single Parent Home				-0.13***	-0.13***	-0.10***	-0.09***
1 Younger Sib				-0.07***	-0.06***	-0.06**	-0.06***
2+ Younger Sibs				-0.17***	-0.15***	-0.13***	-0.12***
1 Older Sib (<18 yrs)				-0.06***	-0.05**	-0.06**	-0.07***
2 Older Sibs (<18 yrs)				-0.12***	-0.09***	-0.11***	-0.11***
3+ Older Sibs (<18 yrs)				-0.23***	-0.19***	-0.20***	-0.20***
Lived in 2 places				-0.04**	-0.04*	-0.03	-0.03
Lived in 3 places				-0.08***	-0.07***	-0.06**	-0.06**
Lived in 4 places				-0.02	-0.01	0.00	0.01
Lived in 5+ places				-0.12***	-0.10***	-0.08**	-0.07*
Large City				0.01	0.01	0.01	0.02
Medium City				-0.05**	-0.05**	-0.05**	-0.05**
Small Town/Rural				-0.17***	-0.13***	-0.11***	-0.11***
Educational Expectations					0.09***	0.08***	0.07***
Center-Based Care					0.21***	0.19***	0.17***
Head Start					0.00	0.01	0.00
Relative Care					0.01	0.02	0.00
Non-Relative Care					0.09***	0.09**	0.07**
Care Varies					0.10**	0.11**	0.09**
Has Home Computer						0.17***	0.15***
Hours of Weekly TV Watching						-0.01	-0.01
Number of Rules about TV Watching						0.01	-0.01
Frequency of Play						-0.03***	-0.03***
Frequency of Reading						0.06***	0.06***
Media [books & tapes (high) vs. TV (low)]						0.09***	0.08***
Arts & Crafts Activities							0.06**
Educational Trips							-0.01
Sports & Clubs							0.06***
Performing Arts							0.12***
Constant	0.20	0.06	0.04	0.24	0.12	0.01	0.01
R^2	0.079***	0.196***	0.257***	0.270***	0.285***	0.301***	0.307***
Change R^2	0.079***	0.117***	0.061***	0.013***	0.015***	0.016***	0.067***

* $p < .05$ ** $p < .01$ *** $p < .001$

Source: Authors' analysis of ECLS-K data.

TABLE 3.2 ECLS-K starting gate: Reading achievement at beginning of kindergarten (n=16,157 children)

	1.	2.	3.	4.	5.	6.	7.
	Race	Social class	Child demographics	Home demographics	Ed. expect. & pre-K care	At-home activities	Outside-home activities
Black	-0.40***	-0.14***	-0.12***	-0.08***	-0.09***	0.01	0.00
Hispanic	-0.45***	-0.23***	-0.16***	-0.17***	-0.17***	-0.12***	-0.12***
Asian	0.30***	0.24***	0.31***	0.29***	0.28***	0.31***	0.32***
Other	-0.40***	-0.24***	-0.23***	-0.17***	-0.16***	-0.11***	-0.11***
Low SES		-0.42***	-0.44***	-0.35***	-0.27***	-0.18***	-0.17***
Low Middle SES		-0.16***	-0.16***	-0.13***	-0.09***	-0.05*	-0.04
High Middle SES		0.25***	0.26***	0.22***	0.19***	0.15***	0.14***
High SES		0.66***	0.67***	0.63***	0.55***	0.46***	0.43***
Female			0.17***	0.17***	0.16***	0.11***	0.07***
Age			0.17***	0.18***	0.18***	0.19***	0.18***
Non-English Home			-0.10***	-0.14***	-0.17***	-0.11***	-0.11**
K-Repeater			0.01	0.00	0.03	0.03	0.03
Fall Test Time			0.09***	0.09***	0.09***	0.08***	0.08***
Single Parent Home				-0.14***	-0.14***	-0.10***	-0.10***
1 Younger Sib				-0.05**	-0.04**	-0.04**	-0.04**
2+ Younger Sibs				-0.14***	-0.12***	-0.11***	-0.10***
1 Older Sib (<18 yrs)				-0.20***	-0.19***	-0.20***	-0.20***
2 Older Sibs (<18 yrs)				-0.32***	-0.29***	-0.31***	-0.30***
3+ Older Sibs (<18 yrs)				-0.41***	-0.36***	-0.37***	-0.37***
Lived in 2 places				-0.03	-0.02	-0.01	-0.01
Lived in 3 places				-0.06**	-0.06**	-0.04*	-0.04*
Lived in 4 places				-0.04	-0.03	-0.02	-0.02
Lived in 5+ places				-0.10**	-0.07*	-0.06	-0.05
Large City				0.02	0.01	0.01	0.01
Medium City				-0.06***	-0.06***	-0.06***	-0.06***
Small Town/Rural				-0.18***	-0.14***	-0.12***	-0.12***
Educational Expectations					0.08***	0.06***	0.06***
Center-Based Care					0.20***	0.18***	0.17***
Head Start					-0.06*	-0.05	-0.06*
Relative Care					-0.02	-0.02	-0.03
Non-Relative Care					0.02	0.02	0.01
Care Varies					0.05	0.05	0.03
Has Home Computer						0.15***	0.14***
Hours of Weekly TV Watching						-0.02**	-0.02*
Number of Rules about TV Watching						0.02	0.02
Frequency of Play						-0.06***	-0.07***
Frequency of Reading						0.13***	0.13***
Media [books & tapes (high) vs. TV (low)]						0.07***	0.06***
Arts & Crafts Activities							0.01
Educational Trips							0.00
Sports & Clubs							0.02
Performing Arts							0.16***
Constant	0.15	-0.03	-0.12	0.17	0.06	-0.04	0.05
R^2	0.045***	0.166***	0.207***	0.232***	0.248***	0.272***	0.277***
Change R^2	0.045***	0.121***	0.041***	0.026***	0.016***	0.024***	0.005***

$* p < .05$ $** p < .01$ $*** p < .001$

Source: Authors' analysis of ECLS-K data.

decline when SES is adjusted for. This suggests how strongly SES is associated with achievement.

Race, SES, and demographics. Taking children's additional demographic characteristics into account further reduces the magnitude of the race and class coefficients on mathematics achievement another 10% to 20%, as the results in step 3 of Table 3.1 indicate. Although gender is unrelated to mathematics achievement at kindergarten entry, children's age, whether they speak English at home, and whether they are repeating kindergarten are. Adding home demographics to the model (step 4) further reduces the magnitude of the race and class coefficients on mathematics achievement. Within the extensive set of variables describing home demographics, several are especially important. Children who have many siblings (either younger or older) have lower mathematics achievement than only children. Children from single-parent homes (-.13 SD) scored below their counterparts with two parents. Those children who experience high residential mobility (effect of -.12 SD) score lower, as do those who reside in a small town or rural area (compared to the suburbs, which has an effect size of -.17 SD).

There is a general pattern in these multivariate models. As the number of explanatory factors in the models increases, the magnitude of the regression coefficients for each is generally not large (because so many other factors are also accounted for). Even when individual effect sizes are rather small in magnitude, together they significantly contribute to achievement. More important to the aim of this report, each helps us understand how race and class actually influence achievement. This is precisely because race and class are related to (i.e., correlated with) the many other demographic and family activities we consider here, as we showed in Chapter 2.

Race, SES, demographics, and child care experience. Though children's experiences in child care the year before kindergarten have some influence on achievement (step 5 of Table 3.1), *they make almost no difference to the magnitude of race effects on mathematics achievement*. They do reduce somewhat the SES gaps, however. Compared to full-time parental care in the home, children who experienced center-based child care before kindergarten show higher achievement (an effect size of .21 SD), as do children whose care was with non-relatives (.09 SD) or who experienced some combination of care (.10 SD). Parents' expectations for their children's education are also positively related to achievement, but the association is small in magnitude (effect size of .09 SD). When parents' expectations and child care experiences are taken into account, the gaps for low vs.

middle SES drops from -0.40 to -.31 SD, and the gap for high vs. middle SES also decreases (from .59 to .51 SD).

Race, SES, demographics, child care, and family activities. After the substantial drop in the magnitude of the coefficients associated with race/ethnicity on math achievement for young children when SES is taken into account, the next most important group of variables in diminishing the size of the race/ethnicity achievement gaps are children's activities with their families in the home (step 6 of Table 3.1). The black/white effect size is reduced by a third, from -.31 to -.21 SD when these factors are taken into account; the magnitude of the Hispanic/white comparison drops 20%, from -.25 to -.20 SD. SES gaps are also reduced by about the same magnitude (e.g., the low vs. middle SES comparison is reduced from -.31 to -.22 SD; the high vs. middle SES comparison drops from .51 to .42 SD). Thus, race and class differences in in-home activities are important for understanding the links between social background and young children's mathematics achievement.

Given that these activities are so important in explaining away social background differences in entry-level achievement, which in-home activities are the most important for achievement? The major impact in this group derives from whether or not the family has a computer at home (effect size of .17 SD). With many other factors taken into account, neither television watching nor rules about TV is statistically associated with mathematics achievement. The final group of explanatory factors include family activities outside the home (step 7 in Table 3.1). In this group, one variable—whether the family exposes the child to performing arts—is most important (.12 SD, a small effect size). However, the magnitude of regression coefficients associated with race and SES are virtually unchanged by taking into account these out-of-home activities.

Explaining variance in math achievement. Although the major focus in these analyses is to investigate which measures (considered in sets) might "explain away" the effect sizes associated with race and class on children's math achievement, it is common to assess the adequacy of statistical models by examining the proportion of variance in the outcome that is accounted for at each step of the model. These results are presented in the bottom section of Table 3.1. The "R^2" figure represents the proportion of total variance explained at each step, whereas the "change in R^2" indicates the additional explanatory power contributed by each step.[15]

Much of this report has focused on the serious disadvantage experienced by children from racial minority groups and from lower-SES fami-

lies in terms of their achievement at school entry, and this phenomenon is underscored by these R^2 figures. For example, taking only children's race/ethnicity into account (step 1) explains 8% of the total variance in math achievement; taking SES into consideration raises the explanatory power of the model to 20% (and the addition of SES to the model adds 11.7% to explained variance). This is quite important: *fully one-fifth of the total variance in math achievement is explained by social background alone.* Adding dozens of additional explanatory factors to the model only raises the proportion of explained variance to 31%. That is, children's race and class—taken alone—are the largest explanatory factors of math achievement.

Comparing social background gaps in math and reading achievement at kindergarten entry

Our discussion of multivariate results in this chapter has, thus far, focused on math achievement. In this section, we examine the full explanatory models for achievement in math and reading by comparing results in Tables 3.1 (mathematics) and 3.2 (reading).

Race gaps alone. Examining the results shown in Tables 3.1 and 3.2 together indicates that the race/ethnicity gaps in reading achievement are somewhat less than in mathematics. For example, unadjusted black/white comparisons are -.40 SD for reading (Table 3.2) and -.62 SD for math (Table 3.1). Although we might expect Hispanic children's disadvantage to be larger for reading than math (given that so many Hispanic children's families do not speak English at home), that is not the case: the Hispanic/white reading deficit is -.45 SD, compared to -.54 SD in mathematics. Surprisingly, Asian children out-score whites in reading by .30 SD, but only by .18 SD in math, even though half of these children live in homes where English is not the main language (see Figure 2.1, panel A). These seemingly anomalous results are understandable when we recall that children whose English-language competency was low were excluded from testing (see endnote 3). Thus, the samples of Hispanic and Asian kindergarten-age children in ECLS-K may be somewhat more selective (especially in terms of English literacy) than children who belong to those racial/ethnic groups who actually began school in 1998.

Race and SES gaps. Even more than in mathematics, race/ethnicity gaps in reading achievement are reduced considerably once SES is taken into account (step 2 in Table 3.2). For example, the black/white gap is reduced 65% (from -.40 to -.14 SD), and the Hispanic/white gap by almost half

(from -.45 to -.23 SD). That is, once SES is taken into account, effect sizes associated with race/ethnicity in reading achievement for children entering kindergarten drop from moderate to small. The magnitude of SES gaps in achievement (adjusted for race) are very similar in reading and math, both being in the moderate to large range. The difference between reading and math is that SES largely explains away the race gaps in reading but is less successful in explaining race differences in math (for both black/white and Hispanic/white comparisons)

Race, SES, and demographics. The pattern of magnitudes of regression coefficients for child demographics is somewhat different between reading and mathematics. For example, although there are no gender differences in math achievement, girls outscore boys by .17 SD in reading achievement at kindergarten entry. The magnitude of the coefficient associated with living in a non-English household is, however, similar in both subjects (-.10 SD). Although there is no difference in reading achievement for those children who do and do not repeat kindergarten, repeaters score lower in math achievement. In general, race/ethnicity gaps on reading are slightly diminished, but SES effect sizes are virtually unchanged, by taking these child demographic factors into account.

When home demographics are accounted for (step 4 in Table 3.1), the black/white gap in math achievement drops by a third (from -.12 to -.08 SD), but the Hispanic and Asian gaps change very little. This difference in changes between the coefficients associated with different racial groups is probably due to single-parent family structure in this step; many more black children live in families with this structure compared to other racial groups (53.7% from panel A in Figure 2.3). Similar for mathematics and reading, achievement scores are considerably lower for children with many siblings (especially older siblings). Also similar for the two achievement measures, children from small towns and rural areas score below their suburban counterparts. High mobility is similarly detrimental to achievement in both subjects. All SES effect sizes in both subjects are reduced somewhat when family demographics are taken into account, mainly because these children's status on these demographic characteristics is associated with their social class.

Race, SES, demographics, and child care experience. Adding child care and parental expectations to the models (step 5 of both Tables 3.1 and 3.2) changes the race and SES gaps in either reading or math achievement very little. Moreover, the effect sizes for these measures are noteworthy. Parents' educational expectations for their children have a small positive ef-

fect size on achievement in both subjects (.09 SD). Center-based child care is moderately and positively associated (.2 SD) with both reading and math achievement compared to parental care only. This type of child care is likely to be a proxy for academically oriented preschool, which may explain the positive result.

Having attended Head Start appears to have a small negative relationship on reading achievement only (-.06 SD), compared to parental care. We note that children's preschool and child care experiences are not strongly associated with achievement in either subject, once social background and demographics are taken into account. It is important to emphasize, however, that neither ECLS-K more generally nor these results in particular should be used to evaluate the effectiveness of children's experiences in preschool and child care in relation to achievement. For example, there is a large volume of research (including some of our own) that demonstrates convincingly that Head Start raises low-income children's cognitive performance substantially. The design of ECLS-K simply does not allow researchers to evaluate the effectiveness of preschool or child care on children's achievement, mainly because the study does not contain information on children's cognitive status as they began preschool or child care. For example, the fact that the coefficients for center-based case are positive and those for Head Start negative in Table 3.1 says absolutely nothing about the effectiveness of these programs. Rather, those coefficients reflect differences in the types of children who are likely to attend these programs, instead of causal effects of the programs on student learning.

Race, SES, demographics, child care, and family activities. Similar to mathematics achievement, in-home activities (step 6 of Table 3.2) decreases the magnitude of racial/ethnic gaps in reading achievement considerably. In fact, *the residual black/white gap in reading achievement has dropped to zero in this model*. The Hispanic/white gap remains (but is reduced in magnitude from -.17 to -.12 SD). Asian children's advantage over whites actually increases a bit at this step, and remains of moderate magnitude (.31 SD in reading, .22 SD in math). The inclusion of in-home activities diminishes considerably the magnitude of SES gaps for reading achievement. For example, the score deficit for low- vs. middle-SES children is diminished by a third (from -.27 to -.18 SD). The advantage of high- vs. middle-SES children declines less (about 20%), from .55 to .46 SD.

The presence of a home computer is equally important for reading and mathematics. Not surprisingly, the frequency of reading at home shows a small but positive effect size (.13 SD), twice as large for reading as for math achievement (.06 SD). The final step in the model, which takes ac-

count of out-of-school activities, does not change the race and SES effect sizes on reading achievement. Similarly to math, children's participation in performing arts has a small positive effect size on reading (.16 SD).

Explaining variance in reading achievement. In one sense, the explanatory model displayed here has been successful, in that *the black/white achievement gap in reading has been completely explained*. The Hispanic/white gap remains, but is greatly reduced. The Asian children's reading advantage over whites, on the other hand, is virtually unaffected by the substantial set of statistical controls in these models. The full model, shown in step 7 of Table 3.2, explains 28% of the variance in reading achievement. In fact, race and SES alone explain somewhat less of the variance in reading achievement (16.6%) than in math (19.6%). Similarly for achievement in reading and mathematics as children enter kindergarten, race and SES are the major explanatory factors.

Summary

Achievement differences among children from different racial groups and differing social classes at the beginning of kindergarten are quite large, as shown in Chapter 1. Moreover, race and SES are associated with other family demographic characteristics and behaviors, as the results in Chapter 2 show. A very important finding from the multivariate analyses in this chapter is that *race/ethnicity gaps in achievement are substantially reduced when children's SES is taken into account*. Much of the deficit in cognitive performance with which Hispanic and black children arrive at the schoolhouse door is due to a simple social phenomenon: black and Hispanic children's families are often poor and their parents less well educated. This simple but striking phenomenon virtually defines social stratification in achievement.

However, these race and class differences in the academic performance of young children are more clearly understood once we account for family demographic factors and academic behaviors in the home. To simplify these complex findings, from the results presented in the top portions of Tables 3.1 and 3.2 we summarize in graphs the effect sizes from each step in the hierarchical regression analyses. **Figure 3.1** summarizes these results by race.

Explaining race differences in achievement. The graphic results in Figure 3.1 show the residual score differences (regression coefficients in effect-size units) in mathematics achievement (panel A) and reading achieve-

FIGURE 3.1   Adjusted race differences, in effect sizes (compared to whites)

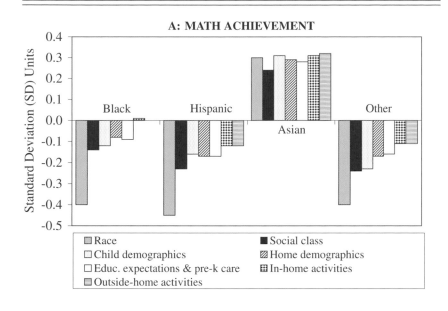

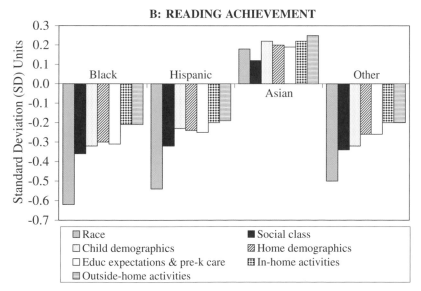

Source: Authors' analysis of U.S. Department of Education ECLS-K data.

ment (panel B) for each racial/ethnic group in comparison to white children. We refer to these differences as "gaps." Comparing the changing lengths of the bars is equivalent to comparing the changing magnitudes of the regression coefficients from Table 3.1. For example, panel A in Figure 3.1 is a visual representation of the successive black/white gaps in math achievement. The seven bars identified as "black" indicate the black/white achievement gaps across the seven steps of the regression models in Tables 3.1 and 3.2, from (1) unadjusted black/white differences to (7) adjusted black/white differences in the full model with all family background and activities included. The fact that these score deficits diminish across the seven bars reflects the fact that the black/white gap shrinks when other factors are considered. From these graphs, and how they change in successive stages, we draw four major conclusions about mathematics and reading achievement as children begin kindergarten:

1.   Even a quick glance at these graphs reveals that the black, Hispanic, and "other" racial groups score below whites (i.e., the bars for each group are below the horizontal axis line), whereas Asian children score above whites (those bars are above).

2.   The multivariate analytic models have been quite successful in explaining away the achievement gaps for blacks, Hispanics, and the other racial group but have not been at all effective in explaining the white/Asian gap. In particular, the black/white gap is greatly reduced, if not eliminated, by adding the additional explanatory factors.

3.   A glance at the graphs reveals that the major single explanation for racial/ethnic gaps between whites and blacks, Hispanics, and the other racial group (but not for the Asian/white comparisons) is SES. The size of the gap changes most dramatically from step 1 to step 2. The second most important explanatory step is in-home activities, especially for black children in comparison with whites.

4.   The patterns of racial/ethnic differences at various stages in our analytic models are quite similar for achievement in reading and mathematics.

Explaining SES differences in achievement.   Differences in achievement for children entering kindergarten by SES are summarized graphically in **Figure 3.2**, again with math achievement in panel A and reading achievement in panel B. Similar to before, these graphs display the changes in the

FIGURE 3.2   Adjusted SES quintile differences, in effect sizes (compared to middle class)

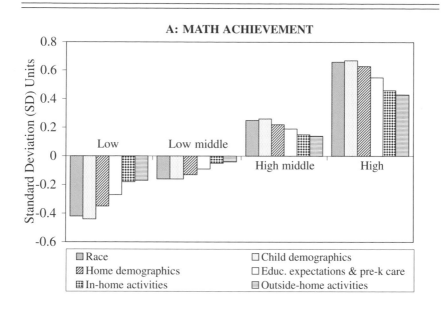

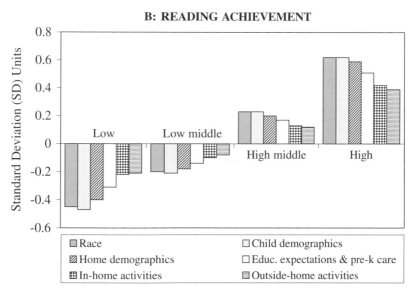

Source: Authors' analysis of U.S. Department of Education ECLS-K data.

SES regression coefficients across the steps of the regression model, from (2) where we estimate SES gaps controlling only for race to (7) where we estimate SES gaps controlling for the entire set of family background and activity measures. Readers are reminded that these comparisons for children of low SES, low-middle SES, high-middle SES, and high SES are to middle class children. At the general level available from this graph, the patterns of results are very similar for the two achievement tests, as was the case for differences by race/ethnicity. We draw five general conclusions from Figure 3.2:

1. The SES gaps shown in Figure 3.2 have already been adjusted for race. Recall from Tables 3.1 and 3.2 that SES was entered at the second step of the regression. That these SES effect sizes are moderate to large, even taking account of race/ethnicity, is an important conclusion.

2. Achievement differences by SES are close to linear, with low and low-middle SES children's achievement below those of middle SES children, and high-middle and high SES children's achievement greater than those of their middle class counterparts.

3. The regression step in which we take other child demographics into account has virtually no effect on the magnitude of SES effect sizes.

4. Each additional step seems to have a roughly equivalent (and small) impact on our ability to "explain away" the relationship between SES and achievement.

5. Although these analytic models were able to explain most of the racial/ethnic achievement gaps (Figure 3.1), the models are less successful in explaining achievement gaps associated with SES (Figure 3.2). For the extreme contrasts (e.g., high vs. middle SES or low vs. middle SES), residual SES effect sizes remain moderate in magnitude (i.e., .2 SD or larger).

The analytic models presented in this chapter take a wide array of demographic factors and family activities into account. *The models are quite successful in explaining race gaps in achievement in mathematics and reading at school entry. However, the models are only moderately successful in explaining social stratification in young children's achievement by SES.* Although the influence of SES is ameliorated when other

family factors are accounted for, the differentiation in achievement by SES is substantial even when a wide array of family demographics and behaviors were included. Social stratification in young children's achievement as they enter school is pervasive and enduring. The analyses in this chapter demonstrate that inequalities in children's educational performance as they begin their formal schooling by family income, parental education, and parents' occupation (the components of SES) are very serious.

In the next chapter, we explore an additional piece of the complex puzzle that captures the starting gate inequalities as they have been demonstrated so far in this report. At the same point in these children's development—beginning kindergarten—all of them are formally enrolled in school, many for the first time. It is unlikely, however, that children of differing social backgrounds experience the same sorts of schooling, even in the earliest years of school. Chapter 4 investigates the *types of schools* children attend as they begin kindergarten, and whether the quality of those schools is associated with the social backgrounds children bring with them to school.

CHAPTER 4

Social disadvantage
and school quality

This chapter explores the types of schools in which all young children begin their formal education in kindergarten. Specifically we investigate whether (and how) the quality of children's first schools is associated with their social background. Consistent with the other chapters, we focus on the time when children start kindergarten, but here we expand on the previous explorations by linking children to schools. Similar to Chapter 3, this chapter's analyses are multivariate rather than descriptive. We define school quality in multiple ways: school sector (whether the school is private or public); kindergarten class size; school outreach to parents; teachers' preparation, experience, and attitudes; school neighborhood conditions; and school social and academic composition. Again, the focus is on children's social background defined in terms of race, ethnicity, and social class and on how these characteristics are linked to the quality of the schools in which they begin kindergarten. This chapter's analyses also take into account a few of the factors considered in Chapter 3: background factors, children's care experiences the previous year, and school location.

Analysis Strategy

Multivariate analyses. Many of the analyses for this chapter make use of the same regression strategy we used in the last chapter. The dependent variables are several measures of school quality measured on a continuous scale. Other analyses, with categorical rather than continuous outcomes, use a statistical technique appropriate for such circumstances: log-linear analysis. Our analytic models are considerably simpler here than those in Chapter 3 (but also more numerous), so none of the multivariate analyses in this chapter are constructed hierarchically. Rather, the coefficients representing the effects associated with each independent variable in the model are estimated simultaneously.

Another difference in this chapter's analyses is how SES is measured. Although our analyses in Chapters 1-3 focused on socioeconomic status

as a composite variable broken into quintiles, here we investigate the influence of the component parts of SES (family income, parents' education, and parents' occupation). In the log-linear analyses, we use a two-level categorical variable as a proxy for family income, coded "1" if the child's family is below the federally defined poverty line (adjusted for family size) and "0" for children who are living at or above the poverty line. In the regression analyses, we consider family income with a continuous variable labeled a "needs ratio."[16] On this measure, *a higher value actually means less need* (and correspondingly more income for a given family size). We also include a measure of the highest level of parents' education, averaging the two if the child lives with both parents or using the single parent's education otherwise. Parents' occupation is coded on a general prestige scale (NCES 2000b), again taking the average if the child lives with both parents. We use the same race/ethnicity categories from the previous chapters. We also include several statistical controls that we introduced in Chapter 2 and used in Chapter 3: the child's gender, whether the child lives in a non-English speaking household, whether the child is repeating kindergarten, his/her preschool or child care experience, and the type of community in which his or her school is located.

Measuring school quality. We recognize that not everyone would agree on exactly which characteristics might constitute a "high-quality school." To address possible disagreements about this, we investigate school quality along 15 different dimensions. We expect that readers may not agree that all of our measures actually represent school quality. For example, some people believe that private schools are better than public schools (but others would not agree), and one of the 15 analyses explores school sector as a measure of school quality (where we compare public, Catholic, other religious, and non-religious private schools).

Most of our measures of school quality, however, are strongly related to school sector, and 85% of the sample of children from ECLS-K used in this report began kindergarten in public school. Therefore, the remainder of the school quality analyses in the chapter focus *only on kindergarten children attending public schools* (reducing the sample in Chapters 1 and 3 of over 16,000 children to over 14,000 children in the analyses in this chapter). Beyond school sector, we grouped the other 14 measures of school quality into the following categories:

- *School social context* (four measures capture average academic skill level, heterogeneity of academic skills, average SES, and heterogeneity of SES);

- *School resources* (seven measures: kindergarten class size, school outreach to parents, kindergarten transition outreach, teachers' preparation, teachers' experience, teachers' collective responsibility, and teachers' professional community); and

- *School environments* (three measures focus on neighborhood problems, problems near the school, and the number of severe problems in the school).

The school quality outcomes we consider are drawn from several sources within the ECLS-K data. The four that define the school social context are drawn from the characteristics of the kindergarten children who attend the school. Average skill level is constructed as the mean of the sum of children's scores on the achievement tests in math and reading at the beginning of kindergarten (the same outcome measures used in Chapter 3). Measures of heterogeneity represent the standard deviation (SD) of either academic skill or SES in each school. Most of the seven measures of school resources are averages of the kindergarten teachers' reports about their schools, their classrooms, their preparation and experience, and their attitudes about their students and colleagues. Reports about school sector, school outreach, and the three measures of school environments were drawn from principals or observers who collected data in each school.[17] (More detail about the school quality measures is in the Appendix.)

Social background and school sector

Each of the three columns of results shown in **Table 4.1** compares the relative likelihood of enrolling in one type of private school as compared to enrolling in public school. The fact that the outcome is a multi-categorical measure dictates that the analyses must be conducted with log-linear methods. Results are, thus, in a *log-odds* rather than an effect-size metric. This means that the substantive interpretation of effect-size magnitudes discussed elsewhere in the report is not applicable here. However, the signs of coefficients indicate a positive or negative likelihood; statistical significance levels rely on the conventional standards.[18] Our discussion centers on differences that are statistically significant. Negative coefficients favor public school enrollment; positive coefficients favor each type of private school.

A major difference between public and private schools is cost: the latter group charges tuition and public schools do not. Another notable difference is that Catholic and other religious school tuition is usually considerably lower than those of other private schools; some schools in the

TABLE 4.1 Social background and school sector: Who has access to private schools? [1]

	Catholic vs. public	Other religious vs. public	Other private vs. public
Social background			
Black	-0.82***	-0.25~	-0.34*
Hispanic	-0.14	-0.60***	-0.23
Asian	-0.21	-0.93**	0.69***
Other	-0.24	-0.28	0.71***
Poverty	-1.07***	-1.75***	-1.10***
Parents' Education	0.39*	0.51**	0.47**
Parents' Occupational Prestige	0.09	-0.04	0.17
Child demographics			
Female	0.09	0.19*	0.17*
Non-English Household	-0.44**	-0.34~	-0.43*
Age	-0.17	-0.08	-0.21
Kindergarten Repeater	0.36~	0.88***	1.30***
Preschool care			
Relative Care [2]	0.47***	0.10	0.39~
Non-Relative Care [2]	0.44***	0.33*	0.64**
Head Start [2]	-0.87***	-2.26***	-0.38
Center-Based Care [2]	0.50***	0.65***	1.31***
Multiple Care [2]	0.29	0.13	0.99***
Urbanicity			
Large City [3]	1.03***	0.93***	0.60***
Medium City [3]	0.66***	0.70***	-0.26*
Rural/Small Town [3]	-0.17	-0.36**	-1.08***
Constant	-3.43***	-4.02***	-3.61***
Likelihood Ratio Chi-Square			1683
Pearson Chi-Square			3854***
Unweighted sample size			16,588

~ $p < .10$ * $p < .05$ ** $p < .01$ *** $p < .001$

[1] Coefficients represent the change in log-odds.
[2] Compared to parental-care only.
[3] Compared to suburban/urban fringe.

Source: Authors' analysis of U.S. Department of Education ECLS-K data.

latter group also have entrance criteria that are more selective than those of religious private schools. Thus, certain social background differences associated with public and private school attendance are not particularly surprising. Black and Hispanic children are more likely to begin kindergarten in public school than white children. For example, black children are considerably less likely than whites to attend either Catholic (change in log-odds of -.82, or a 56% decrease in the odds) or other private schools (change of log-odds of -.34, or a 29% decrease in the odds). Hispanic children are considerably less likely than whites to be in other religious schools (change of log-odds of -.60, or a 45% decrease in the odds), although as likely as whites to attend Catholic schools (presumably because many Hispanics are Catholic). Asian children are much less likely than whites to be enrolled in other religious schools (change in log-odds = -.93, or a 60% decrease in the odds) and more likely than whites to attend other private schools (change in log-odds = .69, or a 99% increase in the odds).

The largest differentiation for attendance at private vs. public school is poverty status. The likelihood of a child in poverty attending any type of private school are very low (change in log-odds over -1.00 for all three comparisons, or a 66%-83% decrease in the odds). Children with more educated parents, on the other hand, are more likely to attend any type of private school than children with less educated parents (a 48%-67% increase in the odds). Preschool experience is also related to elementary school sector, where children who had almost any type of care except Head Start or parent-only care are more likely to attend private than public school; children with Head Start experience are very unlikely to attend private schools (a 90% decrease in the odds for other religious private schools). Comparisons are with in-home parental care in the year before kindergarten.

This pattern of findings for school sector is unsurprising, given cost or tuition differentials and possible selectivity differences. Children from socially disadvantaged backgrounds (defined in terms of their racial/ethnic or poverty status) are more likely than their more advantaged peers to begin their education in public elementary schools. As the vast majority of U.S. kindergartners attend public schools, and because school quality may have different meanings among public and private schools, we restrict our remaining analyses to quality differences among public schools.

Social background and school social context

Table 4.2 shows the results from analyses of four measures of public school social context. Two focus on the academic or skill context of the school (average achievement level and its heterogeneity), and two others focus

on school social class (average SES and its heterogeneity). For analyses of these measures of school quality defined by social context, results are once again in effect-sizes (i.e., standard deviation units), with the same interpretations about magnitudes as in Chapters 1-3. Despite possible disagreement about the meaning of school quality, our interpretation is as follows. Schools of higher average academic skill and higher average SES would be considered by many people to be "higher quality schools," or at least "more advantaged schools." Homogeneity of either skills or SES might be desirable to some parents (especially if the mean is high), however, an especially difficult combination would be schools with homogeneously low-skill or low-SES compositions (even more difficult would be schools homogeneously low on both at the same time). On the other hand, the American ideal of the common school would suggest that heterogeneity is desirable (Cusick 1983). Heterogeneity could also be called "diversity." Although we suspect that some parents and teachers would consider that such diversity leads to problematic environments, we subscribe to the common school ideal.

Race and social context. Although the coefficients associated with SES (especially poverty) were consistently large when examining attendance in public and private schools, the pattern of associations for the several measures of public school social contexts is more striking for race/ethnicity than for various measures of SES. For example, both black and Hispanic children are considerably more likely to attend schools *with lower average academic skill levels.* Black children are also more likely to attend schools that are *more homogeneous in terms of academic skill* than their white counterparts (effect sizes of -.37 SD for both outcomes for blacks; -.40 SD for Hispanics). Compared to whites, Asian children attend higher-skilled schools that are also more heterogeneous. Children in the other racial category evidence the same pattern as blacks. Children who are black, Hispanic, or of other races are also considerably less likely to attend schools characterized by *higher average SES* (effect sizes of -.46, -.30, and -.21 SD, respectively) compared to white children. However, the pattern for school context defined by *SES heterogeneity* is different: black and other children are mapped to more socially heterogeneous schools.

Social class and school context. In the analyses investigating school social context and school resources (Tables 4.2 and 4.3), we define family income as a "needs ratio." Using this interpretation, the results in Table 4.2 indicate that children from families with more economic need are more

TABLE 4.2 Social background and school social context: Who has access to higher quality? [1]

	Average academic skill level	Heterogeneity of academic skill level	Average SES	Heterogeneity of SES
(unweighted sample size)	(14,359)	(14,357)	(14,319)	(14,315)
Social background				
Black	-0.37***	-0.37***	-0.46***	0.31***
Hispanic	-0.40***	-0.15***	-0.30***	-0.02
Asian	0.09*	0.19***	-0.03	0.11
Other	-0.36***	-0.18***	-0.21***	0.15***
Needs Ratio	0.19***	0.10***	0.23***	0.03**
Parents' Education	0.19***	0.14***	0.28***	0.05***
Parents' Occupational Prestige	0.03***	0.02*	0.07***	0.11***
Child demographics				
Female	0.02	-0.02	0.00	0.00
Non-English Household	-0.28***	-0.09**	-0.18***	-0.02
Age	0.09***	0.06***	0.00	0.00
Kindergarten Repeater	-0.12***	-0.08	-0.06~	0.06
Preschool care				
Relative Care [2]	-0.05*	-0.06*	0.00	-0.02
Non-Relative Care [2]	0.09**	0.03	0.10***	-0.01
Head Start [2]	-0.14***	-0.12***	-0.11***	0.14***
Center-Based Care [2]	0.17***	0.09***	0.12***	0.05
Multiple Care [2]	0.04	0.04	0.02	0.03
Urbanicity				
Large City [3]	-0.31***	-0.14***	-0.43***	0.12***
Medium City [3]	-0.36***	-0.15***	-0.29***	0.11***
Rural/Small Town [3]	-0.47***	-0.36***	-0.42***	0.14***
Constant	0.18***	0.14***	0.13***	-0.19***
R-squared	0.38***	0.15***	0.48***	0.04***

* $p < .05$ ** $p < .01$ *** $p < .001$

[1] All outcomes and continuous predictors are z-scores.
[2] Compared to parental-care only.
[3] Compared to suburban/urban fringe.

Source: Authors' analysis of U.S. Department of Education ECLS-K data.

likely to attend schools with less skilled children (effect size of .19 SD), with a similar pattern for school-SES (effect size of .23 SD). However, children whose parents are more educated are more likely to attend higher-skilled and higher-SES schools (effects of .19 and .28 SD).

Other background characteristics and school social context. Although our focus in this report is on race/ethnicity and SES as defining characteristics of social background, a few other patterns shown in Table 4.2 are noteworthy. For example, children from non-English speaking households, those living in large cities and in rural areas (compared to the suburbs), or those whose preschool experience was in Head Start were also more likely to attend schools defined by less advantaged contexts, that is, lower skilled and lower SES, and more homogeneous in both respects. Thus, other patterns of disadvantage are consistent with the racial, ethnic, and social class focus of special interest in this report. Regression models that focus on average academic skill and average SES are quite well explained, where 38% and 48% of the variance in these two outcomes is explained, respectively.

Social background and school resources

Seven different measures of school resources are examined in **Table 4.3**, which define several different types of resources. We investigate a standard resource measure, *kindergarten class size*, with smaller class sizes representing higher quality. Two measures capture schools' outreach to parents: one considers *general outreach*, the other capturing more specific issues of outreach that are meant to *ease the child's sometimes difficult transition into kindergarten*. Two measures define quality in terms of teachers' qualifications: their *academic preparation* (coursework, degrees) and their *experience teaching kindergarten and other grades*. Two other resource measures are defined by teachers' attitudes: one focuses on teachers' reports of their *willingness to take responsibility for their students' learning* (what we call "collective responsibility"), the other taps teachers' reports about *community with their professional colleagues* (what we call "professional community").[19] We discuss the outcomes capturing school resources in logical groupings. In general, the school quality measures defined by resources are not well explained by these models, except for kindergarten transition outreach (where 18% of the variance is explained).

Kindergarten class size. Findings here are straightforward. Compared to their white counterparts, children who are black, Hispanic, or Asian are enrolled in schools with larger kindergarten classes. Children of other racial backgrounds are in smaller classes, perhaps because of the high proportion of Native American children in this group attending small reservation schools. Children with families with more economic need also attend schools with larger kindergarten classes, as do (somewhat unexpectedly)

TABLE 4.3 Social background and school resources: Who has access to higher quality? [1]

	Kindergarten class size	General school-parent outreach	Kindergarten transition outreach	Teachers' preparation	Teachers' experience	Teachers' collective responsibility	Teachers' professional community
(Unweighted sample size)	(12,601)	(11,985)	(14,147)	(13,753)	(13,865)	(14,147)	(14,105)
Social background							
Black	0.61***	0.22***	-0.48***	-0.14***	-0.14***	-0.31***	-0.11***
Hispanic	0.49**	0.07*	-0.37***	-0.19***	-0.09**	-0.07*	-0.05
Asian	0.73*	0.04	-0.19***	-0.13*	-0.10	0.05	0.08
Other	-0.81***	0.14**	-0.50***	-0.02	-0.25***	-0.16***	-0.19***
Needs ratio	-0.11*	0.03**	0.08***	0.02	0.00	0.04***	0.02*
Parents' education	0.12*	0.02	0.05	0.06***	0.05***	0.10***	0.10***
Parents' occupational prestige	0.00	0.02	-0.01	0.01	-0.03**	-0.01	0.00
Child demographics							
Female	0.09	-0.02	0.02	-0.02	0.01	0.01	0.00
Non-English household	0.11	-0.11**	-0.25***	-0.11***	-0.14***	0.03	-0.03
Age	-0.14**	0.01	0.06***	0.03**	0.02**	0.02	0.00
Kindergarten repeater	-0.06	0.05	-0.08	0.01	-0.13**	-0.04	0.08
Preschool care							
Relative care [2]	0.06	-0.04	-0.02	-0.01	0.02	0.05	-0.01
Non-relative care [2]	0.05	-0.08*	0.03	-0.05	0.05	0.01	-0.08*
Head Start [2]	-0.19	0.09**	0.02	0.06	-0.04	-0.06	-0.02
Center-based care [2]	-0.07	0.02	0.03	-0.02	0.01	-0.01	-0.01
Multiple care [2]	-0.55**	0.04	0.07	-0.01	0.04	-0.03	-0.11**

(cont.)

TABLE 4.3 *(cont.)* **Social background and school resources: Who has access to higher quality?** [1]

	Kindergarten class size	General school-parent outreach	Kindergarten transition outreach	Teachers' preparation	Teachers' experience	Teachers' collective responsibility	Teachers' professional community
(Unweighted sample size)	(12,601)	(11,985)	(14,147)	(13,753)	(13,865)	(14,147)	(14,105)
Urbanicity							
Large city [3]	0.89***	0.15***	-0.40***	0.20***	0.01	-0.31***	-0.37***
Medium city [3]	-1.42***	0.25***	-0.09***	0.05*	0.03	-0.13***	0.04
Rural/small town [3]	-0.93***	0.04	0.24***	-0.07**	0.11***	-0.13***	-0.34***
Constant	21.3***	-0.12***	0.23***	0.07**	0.03	0.18***	0.19***
R-squared	0.04***	0.02***	0.18***	0.02***	0.02***	0.06***	0.06***

* p < .05   ** p < .01   *** p < .001

[1] All outcomes (except for kindergarten class size) and continuous predictors are z-scores.
[2] Compared to parental-care only.
[3] Compared to suburban/urban fringe.

Source: Authors' analysis of U.S. Department of Education ECLS-K data.

children with more educated parents. The strongest associations here refer to location. Compared to the suburbs, children attending schools in urban areas are in much larger kindergarten classes, whereas children in schools in medium cities and rural areas are in smaller classes.

School outreach*.* General school outreach seems to be more common for children attending schools in large and medium-sized cities, and for children attending schools enrolling more black and non-English speaking children (see column 2 of Table 4.3). However, perhaps a more useful form of outreach for young children, where school staff help parents ease their children's transition into kindergarten, is quite uncommon for children who are black, Hispanic, Asian, other races, and children from non-English households (column 3). Compared to the suburbs, children in schools in large and medium-sized cities are less likely to have access to this type of outreach, although those in rural and small-town schools apparently do. Family income is related to this type of outreach, with children with more need being slightly less likely to attend such schools. The largest associations are for race/ethnicity and school location. Minority children's parents, especially those residing in cities, are especially unlikely to experience outreach of this type, even though they might benefit from it quite a lot.

Teacher quality*.* Minority kindergartners attend schools with less prepared teachers, although after taking race/ethnicity into account, economic need is unrelated to teacher preparation (column 4 of Table 4.3). However, young children with more educated parents attend schools where teachers are better prepared. The same pattern is evident for schools characterized by more experienced teachers. Not everyone would agree that more teacher experience makes a higher quality school (nearly half the nation's kindergarten teachers have been teaching at least 15 years). Minority children and those from non-English households attend schools whose teachers have less experience (Column 5). Kindergartners with more educated parents, however, attend schools with more experienced teachers. Neither economic need, preschool care, nor school location is related to teacher experience, with one exception: children attending rural schools have teachers who are more experienced (but less well prepared).

Teacher attitudes*.* We include measures of professional community and teachers' attitudes about collective responsibility here because empirical research has linked these to achievement and learning for older children. For example, Lee and her colleagues found that more collective responsi-

bility was linked to higher achievement gain among students in the middle grades (Lee and Loeb 2000) and in high school (Lee and Smith 1996). Louis and her colleagues (1996a, 1996b) defined school professional community and demonstrated its link with achievement across grade levels.

Results in columns 6 and 7 of Table 4.3 indicate that black children attend schools characterized by lower levels of both collective responsibility (effect size of -.31 SD) and professional community (effect size of -.11 SD). On the other hand, more-advantaged children (i.e., those whose parents have more income and more education) are more likely to attend schools defined by these positive attitudes among kindergarten teachers. Beyond race and class, the most consistent findings here relate to school location. Compared to the suburbs, the schools attended by children in both city and rural schools are characterized by less positive teacher attitudes.

Social background and school environment

Analytic strategy. The three measures of environmental conditions shown in **Table 4.4** are categorical contrasts, because distributions of variables defining these school conditions are highly skewed (i.e., bad conditions are unusual). The categories in the three measures—*neighborhood problems surrounding the school* (e.g., substance abuse, gangs, heavy traffic, crime, unoccupied buildings), *bad conditions near school* (e.g., trash, graffiti, boarded up buildings), and *severe problems within the schools* (e.g., weapons, theft, attacks)—are defined so that each is a comparison with the category just below it in terms of severity (the Appendix defines these measures more completely). Analyses here again use log-linear methods, so that coefficients in Table 4.4 are in the same log-odds metric used in the results in Table 4.1. We focus discussion on the direction, statistical significance, and relative magnitude of results.

Social background and school environmental conditions. Results for social background here are straightforward: black, Hispanic, and children of other races are more likely than their white counterparts to attend public schools located in neighborhoods characterized by problem conditions (column 1 of Table 4.4). The same pattern is evident for children from families living in poverty and those who attended Head Start. Unsurprisingly, children attending schools in large cities (and, to a lesser extent, in medium-sized cities) experience the most problematic neighborhoods (as compared to children attending schools in the suburbs). Children attending rural schools are less likely to experience problematic neighborhoods.

TABLE 4.4 Social background and school environments: Who is exposed to bad conditions?[1]

	Neighborhood problems surrounding school			Bad conditions near school		Severe problems inside school	
	Slight vs. none	Small vs. slight	Some/Big vs. small	Very Little vs. none	Some vs. very little	One vs. none	Two/Three vs. one
Social background							
Black	-0.11	0.78***	0.55***	0.30***	1.87***	0.19**	-0.08
Hispanic	0.00	0.31***	0.79***	0.24**	1.22***	-0.21**	0.07
Asian	-0.20	-0.21	0.41	0.37*	0.68**	0.05	-0.41
Other	0.35**	0.49***	1.58***	0.46***	1.81***	0.19	0.24
Poverty	0.01	0.25***	0.25***	0.22**	0.30**	0.05	0.05
Parents' education	-0.18~	-0.10	0.05	-0.06	0.00	0.17	0.03
Parents' occupational prestige	0.00	-0.06	-0.01	0.00	-0.31**	0.14	0.26*
Child demographics							
Female	-0.06	-0.02	0.01	0.01	-0.15*	-0.01	0.03
Non-English Household	0.40***	-0.02	0.29**	0.28**	0.08	0.19*	-0.12
Age	0.02	-0.03	-0.13	-0.11	0.00	-0.08	-0.16*
Kindergarten Repeater	-0.09	-0.15	0.37*	0.34**	0.02	-0.07	0.27
Preschool care							
Relative Care [2]	0.08	-0.08	0.34**	0.01	0.05	-0.12	0.02
Non-Relative Care [2]	-0.04	-0.28**	0.11	-0.06	-0.32*	-0.02	0.14
Head Start [2]	-0.34***	0.35***	0.29*	0.21*	0.18	-0.26**	0.23*
Center-Based Care [2]	-0.10	-0.27***	0.40**	-0.07	-0.12	-0.11	0.22*
Multiple Care [2]	-0.03	-0.11	0.45*	-0.14	0.15	-0.16	0.34**
Urbanicity							
Large City [3]	0.41***	0.53***	1.08***	1.08***	1.23***	-0.18**	1.04***
Medium City [3]	0.20**	0.28***	0.92***	0.26***	0.77***	-0.27***	0.96***
Rural/Small Town [3]	-0.17**	0.04	-0.63***	-0.07	0.38***	-0.32***	0.68***
Constant	0.82***	-0.77***	-0.18	0.15	-0.84***	-0.28***	-0.62***

Likelihood			
Ratio Chi-Square	3452***	2464***	2501***
Pearson Chi-Square	3488***	2419***	2298***
Unweighted sample size	10,903	11,681	10,979

* p < .05   ** p < .01   *** p < .001

[1] Coefficients represent the change in log-odds.
[2] Compared to parental-care only.
[3] Compared to suburban/urban fringe.

Source: Authors' analysis of U.S. Department of Education ECLS-K data.

The same pattern is even more evident for poor conditions immediately surrounding the elementary schools (column 2 of Table 4.4), as the log-odds coefficients for all the racial minority groups, compared to whites are fairly large, positive, and statistically significant. Black children are over five times more likely than white children to encounter at least some bad conditions near school (change in log-odds 1.87). Children attending schools in large cities are nearly three times more likely than children attending schools in the suburbs to encounter at least some bad conditions near school (change in log-odds=1.23). Quite simply, children from families in poverty (especially in urban areas) are considerably more likely to attend schools located in neighborhoods with problems.

Although results in the first two outcomes of Table 4.4 describe associations between social background and problems in the neighborhoods and areas around the school, results in column 3 describe problems within the schools. These are elementary schools, so problems with weapons, theft, and attacks are far less common than in schools enrolling older children. Thus, there are few effects of social background here. The major finding is that kindergartners entering elementary schools in large cities, medium-sized cities, and rural areas are all significantly more likely to be exposed to these within-school problems than suburban schools (a 97%-182% increase in the odds).

Summary

In this chapter we explore how young children's social background is linked to the quality of the elementary schools where they begin kindergarten. Although race/ethnicity and socioeconomic status (particularly defined by poverty or economic need) are not equally strongly associated with school quality across the many different dimensions on which we measured it, *the patterns of association are themselves strikingly consistent.*[20] Considering almost every way we measured school quality, children who belong to racial minority groups (most strongly for blacks but also for Hispanics and the "other" racial group), begin their formal schooling in lower quality schools than their white counterparts. *Whether defined by less favorable social contexts, larger kindergarten classes, less outreach to smooth the transition to first grade, less well-prepared and experienced teachers, less positive attitudes among teachers, or poor neighborhood and school conditions, children from less advantaged social backgrounds begin elementary school in lower-quality institutions.* The consistency of these findings, across aspects of school quality that are themselves very different from one another, is both striking and troubling. The least advantaged of

America's children, who also begin their formal schooling at a substantial cognitive disadvantage, are systematically mapped into our nation's worst schools.

Another consistency is the strong association between the type of communities where schools are located (large or medium-sized city, suburbs, small town, or rural area) and the quality of their public schools. The lowest quality schools are in America's large cities. Not quite so consistent, but still striking, is that low-quality schools—as defined by many measures we investigated here—also typify the educational institutions in small towns and rural areas. The highest quality schools are located in the suburbs, where the most affluent citizens reside.

CHAPTER 5

Conclusions and policy recommendations

At the starting gate

This report is about education but it is not about schooling. Our purpose has been to explore the degree to which social inequalities exist among young children as they begin their formal schooling in kindergarten. Much has been written about socially based achievement differences for children in school, and how these inequalities are magnified by children's experiences in the educational process. These writings lay much of the blame for social stratification in educational outcomes on the schools—often implicating low-quality teaching and discriminatory practices like ability grouping and tracking that are differentially allocated to students based on social and academic background.

This report documents problems that all educational professionals—teachers and school administrators—recognize and many confront: Even the youngest children present themselves at the doors of their schoolhouses and classrooms with enormous variation in their cognitive and social skills. We explored how these cognitive skills, defined by achievement test scores in mathematics and reading administered at the beginning of kindergarten, are associated with young children's race, ethnicity, and social class. Using recent data that are almost ideal for exploring these questions—the Early Childhood Longitudinal Study (ECLS-K) from the U.S. Department of Education—we show here that children's social background characteristics are strongly associated with academic competence as they begin school.

Beyond race and class, many other demographic characteristics of young children and their families, as well as children's own care experiences and activities with their families in and out of the home, are associated with academic achievement at school entry. These family characteristics and behaviors also differ considerably by race and class. Thus, when these factors are taken into account, the observed differences in achievement by race and class are reduced, and in some cases explained away. But even so, race and class differences are nonetheless real.

When statistical adjustments account for the observed achievement differences, that only means that race and class are associated with other phenomena that are related to achievement. Hence, we are only explaining away what researchers call the *direct effect* of race and class. If race and class are significantly associated with other behaviors and experiences which are themselves significantly related to early cognitive status, then a direct effect of race and class has simply been replaced by an *indirect effect* of race and class. One interpretation of these findings is that race or class alone are incomplete in describing social disadvantage in cognitive competence.

Beyond considering home-based activities, child care experiences, and demographic factors beyond race and class, we investigated how social background is associated with the quality of the schools where children begin their educational experiences in kindergarten. Findings here are straightforward, consistent, and sobering. Regardless of how we define school quality (by the social or academic composition of the school; whether it is public or private; the size of its classes; its outreach to parents; the preparation or attitudes of its teachers; or the conditions that surround it), the least-advantaged children attend public elementary schools of the lowest quality. Access to high-quality schools in the U.S. is strongly associated with children's social background—either directly or indirectly— through the communities in which they reside and where their schools are located. In addition to the explorations in other chapters that have demonstrated the link between social inequality and children's opportunities to learn out of school, the findings from Chapter 4 demonstrate a conclusive link between social background and the quality of the schools children attend in kindergarten.

Social policy considerations

Were this report to have focused on how U.S. children fare in their schools once they were enrolled, formulating social policy recommendations that focus on how schools are run and how they serve the children they are charged with educating would be straightforward. We would then discuss the changes schools should make to increase opportunities to learn for disadvantaged children. Because our focus is on children and their families at the point when these young children enter school, school-based social policy recommendations are inappropriate. Nevertheless, our results suggest some obvious and not-so-obvious social policy implications.

Race, class, and cognitive status are intertwined. Our findings confirm a very disturbing phenomenon in American society: that the parents of chil-

dren who are members of certain minority groups—particularly blacks and Hispanics—occupy the lowest rungs on the income and education ladders in the U.S. This is, of course, not news. We emphasize this linkage precisely because it indicates that most minority children come to school with a double disadvantage. Results in Chapter 3 demonstrate that double disadvantage very vividly: Almost half of the racial/ethnic gaps in achievement is explained by taking children's social class into account. Our analyses, in fact, indicate that none of the many other factors we considered come close to explaining as much of the race-based achievement gaps as does social class. Other factors that determine family disadvantage or that put children at risk of school failure—single-parent family structure, family size, high residential mobility, residence in large cities and rural areas—are also disproportionately allocated to poor and minority children and their families.

Over the last decade or two, the U.S. has experienced growing income disparities—the rich have gotten much richer, which means that the poor are poorer (by comparison, if not in absolute terms). Economists and social scientists have attested that the growing income disparity is due, in large part, to such American social policies as shrinking social safety nets, increasingly regressive tax codes, continuing public support for home ownership at the expense of renters, and welfare reform. Because such a large proportion of the poor are minority children, growing income disparities have serious implications for children's socially differentiated school performance defined in cognitive and social terms. As a nation, we continue to support the role—even the obligation—of schooling to close these gaps, but at the same time we create or magnify the same gaps with other social policies. Except for continuing support for Head Start (actually a relatively inexpensive program), our public policies do little to address the negative educational effects that income disparities have on young children. The U.S. should not use one hand to blame the schools for inadequately serving disadvantaged children when its social policies have helped to create these disadvantages—especially income disadvantages—with the other hand.

Family size and structure. Although we do not suggest that social policies should be targeted directly at parents' own decisions about the size and structure of their families, our findings do suggest how important these factors are in determining young children's cognitive status. Compared to being an only child, having any siblings is a disadvantage. Although having two or more younger siblings translates into lower achievement, we were surprised to find that the most negative family configuration is actu-

ally for a child who is the youngest with many older siblings. For achievement in reading, even in the final analytic models in Chapter 3, this is one of the most important single factors beyond race and social class.

Child care and preschool. Obviously, whether children come to kindergarten with educational preparation in preschool plays a role in their academic and social competence at that point. Although results in Chapter 3 indicate that child care experiences (along with parents' educational expectations for their children) actually change race/ethnicity effects very little, they do explain away SES gaps to some degree. One type of child care, however, seems more important than the others: center-based care. We can only assume that this measure captures what we commonly think of as preschools with some academic content, although the ECLS-K dataset does not allow us to validate this assumption. We cautioned elsewhere that our analyses cannot be used as *evaluations* of the efficacy of preschool programs and provided a rationale for this position. However, we believe it is still appropriate to draw some policy implications about the importance of preschool preparation, although we admit that these policy lessons are at best speculative. It seems quite obvious that a major way to reduce social inequalities in children's cognitive status (and social competence) as they begin kindergarten is through disadvantaged children's participation in well-designed preschool preparation programs with at least some academic content.

Many disadvantaged children already experience publicly funded preschool programs, through either state programs or the federally funded Head Start program (even though most do not). We believe, however, that the nation's investments in such programs need to be increased enormously; Figures 2.7 and 2.8 suggest that *less than half of our nation's least-advantaged kindergartners* (children from the lowest SES quintile) had been enrolled in either center-based preschool (about 20%) or a Head Start program (about 27%). More advantaged children regularly experience such preschool programs (nearly two-thirds of the most affluent children had been enrolled in center-based preschool), but access to these programs is limited by their high tuitions (particularly if they are coupled with full-day child care) and by their location (many fewer are located in areas where less advantaged children actually reside). Why should only advantaged children have access to the strongest programs? The fact that center-based child care shows positive benefits compared to full-time parental care suggests that such programs may be valuable for all children. We suspect that the preschool experiences in center-based programs may contain more academic content than those in Head Start.

We would need a more fine-grained study that compares several types of preschool (including information about their curricula, their staff qualifications, and their student's cognitive status at preschool entry), compared to no preschool at all, to validate this speculation. We underscore, nevertheless, that a full-day preschool and child care experience of high quality that was available to children regardless of their parents' ability to pay and was physically accessible to low-income families would benefit the most disadvantaged children very much. Much of the effort to improve Head Start over time has focused more on *expanding access* to the program than to *improving its intensity or quality*. Even so, with so many poor kindergartners who experienced neither center-based preschool nor Head Start, the expansion of Head Start, however successful, is far from complete. Moreover, it is well known that high-quality preschool education has been shown to have solid and lasting benefits to the disadvantaged young children who are fortunate enough to have experienced it. The major problem, we suggest, is that so few disadvantaged children have access to such programs.

Computers at home.   Beyond the importance of social background and family demographics in determining children's cognitive status, the strongest single link with achievement in our models is the presence or absence of a computer in the home (regardless of its use). This is an important, if possibly controversial, finding. We speculate that the single measure of computer ownership is actually a proxy for a more *educationally rich* home environment. Why do parents buy computers for home use? Obviously, some do so to facilitate and continue their work at home. Some parents receive training for computer usage in the workplace, so they can exercise this expertise in buying, setting up, and using a computer at home. Self-employed parents may use them for bookkeeping, billing, and word processing. More and more information is available on the Internet; access to the Internet and e-mail is surely a major motivation for owning a computer. Many parents surely purchase home computers primarily for their children. Although some adults have not yet entered the computer age (and some are quite resistant), computer usage is ubiquitous for most children in school.

Our evidence is that computer ownership and usage is race and class based, surely for reasons of costs and motivation. Schools with more resources spend some of them on buying and updating computers, on software to operate them, and on staff to train teachers and students. Moreover, parents and older siblings model computer usage at home, so that children want to emulate this behavior. We stop far short of advocating a

social policy that would put a computer in every child's home, regardless of race and class. This type of policy would not necessarily diminish social stratification in children's academic performance. However, our findings here offer support for the often-cited phenomenon of "the digital divide." The presence of a computer in the home is important to young children's achievement even before they start school.

Disadvantage and school quality

The findings in this report with perhaps the clearest social policy implications concern school quality. Across a wide and diverse array of school quality measures, social background is consistently linked to the quality of schools children attend. The poorest children in economic terms, those from black and Hispanic families, from families where parents are less educated, and children attending schools in large cities and rural areas attend the lowest quality schools. Whether "quality" is defined in terms of school sector, class size, school outreach to parents, teacher qualifications, teacher attitudes, or school environmental conditions, disadvantaged and minority children begin their educational careers in schools of consistently lower quality. Those findings translate into a sobering conclusion: The children who need the best schooling actually start their education in the worst public schools.

Why, however, is this linked to policy? Which social policies might influence the mapping of poor children to poor public schools? Two are obvious candidates. First, school finance. To a large degree our nation's public schools are financed by local property taxes. Schools in poor communities, in cities and towns with many low-income residents, have the lowest resource bases. Although federal policies such as Title I are meant to ameliorate these disparities, the proportion of total funding for public schooling that comes from federal sources is quite small: about 5%-10%. Local property taxes typically finance about 45%-50%, with another 45%-50% coming from the state. Although some states have begun to direct slightly more funding to low-income districts, higher-income districts loudly and consistently resist this trend as unfair. In some schools with funding shortfalls, more and more services that used to be provided by public schools free of charge (art, music, after-school activities, and some sports) are now provided to children whose parents are willing and able to pay for them. This effectively denies low-income parents access to such services, as their schools are perhaps the most likely to experience shortfalls.

The second social policy recommendation is related to the first. Historically and currently, there is a widespread belief that access, or assign-

ment, to schooling should be local, and that children (especially young children) benefit from attending schools close to their homes. Other social policies have led to extremes in social and racial stratification in residential location in this country. Thus, the policy of local access to schooling automatically leads to low-quality schooling for residents of low-income areas.

Readers are strongly urged not to interpret these conclusions as lending support for vouchers or school choice, which is not at all what is being advocated. Research (including our own) has shown that *increased choice almost always results in more social stratification in educational programs and outcomes, not less* (see, e.g., Bryk and Lee 1992; Lee 1993; Lee, Croninger, and Smith 1994). The weight of this entire report highlights problems of inequality. We care so much about educational equity that we would support no social policies or programs that increase social stratification in educational outcomes. Rather, we support a more equitable distribution of children across public schools. Moreover, we support policies that seek to improve all schools, so access to good schools is not confined to the affluent, to whites, to those who reside in the suburbs, or to those who are well enough informed to seek them out. We argue that public schooling is the nation's number one social intervention. As such, equity should be at the top of the list of criteria. We should not allow school location to determine school quality, nor should we rely on choice that allows only *some* low-income parents to gain access to high-quality schools for their children, often at the expense of those whom they leave behind. *All* schools should be high-quality schools and *all* children should attend such schools.

Final thoughts

It is important to recognize that, although we may use statistical methodology to "adjust" the links between children's race, ethnicity, and social class and their achievement scores, the major purpose of these adjustments is to indicate that family characteristics and activities are linked with both achievement and social background. Such "adjusted demographics" are not how children present themselves to schools. The multiple disadvantages of minority status—low income, low parental education, perhaps single-parent status, and a lack of educational resources in the home—are the realities that their kindergarten teachers and schools must confront.

We have documented in this report that there is much diversity in the academic skills young children bring to school as they begin. Much of this diversity in performance is linked to children's social background, par-

ticularly to race and social class. Some family demographics and activities explain these race- and class-based performance differences, but statistics aside, those differences remain and are every day observable in the classroom. Schools face a tremendous challenge in how to accommodate this diversity, so that each child can be successful in school. However, the findings in this report document that the children who need the very best schools—those who are poor and in the ethnic minority—actually begin their formal schooling in American public schools of the lowest quality. We cannot blame the schools for this mapping, but neither is it purely accidental. It is important that American citizens both recognize this unfortunate phenomenon and make serious and sustained efforts to correct it.

Appendix of measures

Entering Achievement:

Fall Math Score – Standardized (IRT-scaling) test of math achievement [from C1MSCALE], an untimed, individually administered cognitive test of achievement.

Fall Reading Score – Standardized (IRT-scaling) test of reading achievement [from C1RSCALE], an untimed, individually administered cognitive test of achievement.

Social Background:

Black – Dummy coded race variable, 1=Black, 0=Other [recoded from RACE].

Hispanic – Dummy coded race variable, 1=Hispanic, 0=Other [recoded from RACE].

Asian – Dummy coded race variable, 1=Asian, 0=Other [recoded from RACE].

Other – Dummy coded race variable, 1="Other," 0=Other [recoded from RACE].

SES – Z-score, mean=0, SD=1, continuous composite measure of socioeconomic status (including parents' education, parents' occupational prestige, and household income) [from WKSESL], also collapsed into quintiles [from WKSESQ5] and represented by four-coded measures comparing low SES (first quintile), low middle SES (second quintile), high middle SES (fourth quintile), and high SES (fifth quintile) to middle SES (third quintile).

Needs Ratio – Continuous measure of family income and household composition, 1 = at US government-defined poverty level, 2 = at twice the US-defined poverty level, 3=at three times the US government-defined poverty level, etc. [from WKINCOME, P2LESS18, P2OVER18, and P2HTOTAL].

Poverty – Dummy coded poverty status indicator, 1=Below Poverty Level, 0=At or above poverty level [from WKPOVRTY].

Parents' Education – Parents' highest level of education in years [from WKPARED].

Parents' Occupational Prestige – Average occupational prestige of parents, reflecting the 1989 General Social Survey prestige score [from WKMOMSCR & WKDADSCR].

Child Demographics:

Female – Dummy coded gender variable, 1=Female, 0=Male [recoded from GENDER].

Non-English Household – Dummy coded family background variable, 1=English is not the home language, 0=English is the home language [recoded from WKLANGST].

Kindergarten Repeater – Dummy coded student enrollment indicator, 1=Child is repeating kindergarten, 0=Child is a first-time kindergartner [recoded from P1FIRKDG].

Age – Z-score, Mean=0, (SD)=1, child's age (in months) in September 1998 [from date of birth information: DOBMM, DOBYY].

Fall Testing Time – Z-score, Mean=0, (SD)=1, time (in days) from September 1 to the Fall testing date [from C1ASMTMM, C1ASMTDD.].

Home Demographics:

Single Parent Household – Dummy coded family structure indicator, 1=Single Parent Household, 0=Two Parent Household [recoded from P1HFAMIL].

Number of Younger Siblings – Number of children in household whose age is less than the age of the ECLS–K kindergartner [computed from AGE and the ages of the household members (the P1AGE_3 to P1AGE_18 series)], collapsed into three groups (no younger siblings, one younger sibling, two or more younger siblings), and represented by two dummy coded measures comparing kindergartners with one younger sibling and two or more younger siblings to kindergartners with no younger siblings.

Number of older siblings – Number of children in household (under 18 years of age) whose age is equal to or greater than the age of the ECLS-K kindergartner [computed from AGE and the ages of the household members (the P1AGE_3 to P1AGE_18 series)], collapsed into four groups (no older siblings, one older sibling, two older siblings, three or more younger siblings), and represented by three dummy coded measures comparing kindergartners with one older sibling, two older siblings, and three or more older siblings to kindergartners with no older siblings.

Number of Places Lived – Number of places the child has lived (for at least 4 months) since the child was born [from P1NUMPLA], collapsed into five categories, and represented by four dummy variables comparing kindergartners who lived in two, three, four, and five or more places to kindergartners who lived in only one place.

Large City – Dummy coded urbanicity indicator, 1=Large city, 0=Other [recoded from KURBAN]. A large city is defined as a central city of a Consolidated Metropolitan Statistical Area (CMSA) with a population greater than or equal to 250,000.

Medium City – Dummy coded urbanicity indicator, 1=Medium city, 0=Other [recoded from KURBAN]. A medium, or mid-sized, city is defined as a central city of a MCSA or Metropolitan Statistical Area (MSA) with a population less than 250,000.

Small Town/Rural – Dummy coded urbanicity indicator, 1=Small town or rural, 0=Other [recoded from KURBAN]. A small town is an incorporated place or Census Designated Place with a population less than 25,000 and greater than 2,5000, located outside a CMSA or MSA. A rural locale is any incorporated place, Census Designated Place, or non-place territory designated as rural by the Census Bureau.

Educational Expectations and Primary Pre-Kindergarten Care:

Parents' Educational Expectations for Child – Z-score, Mean=0, (SD)=1, continuous measure of parents' educational expectations for child (highest degree expected), originally coded from 1= less than high school diploma to 6=Ph.D., MD or other higher degree [from P1EXPECT].

Relative Care – dummy coded pre-kindergarten primary care indicator, 1=Relative care (in home or in relative's home), 0=other [recoded from P1PRIMPK].

Non-Relative Care – dummy coded pre-kindergarten primary care indicator, 1=Non-relative care (in home or in non-relative's home), 0=other [recoded from P1PRIMPK].

Head Start – dummy coded pre-kindergarten primary care indicator, 1=Head Start, 0=other [recoded from P1PRIMPK].

Center-Based Care – dummy coded pre-kindergarten primary care indicator, 1=Center-based care, 0=other [recoded from P1PRIMPK].

Multiple Care – dummy coded pre-kindergarten primary care indicator, 1=Primary care varies, 0=other [recoded from P1PRIMPK].

AT-Home Activities:

Home Computer Ownership – Dummy coded measure indicating the presence of a home computer, 1=home computer, 0=no home computer [recoded from P2HOMECM].

Weekly Hours of TV Watching – Z-score, Mean=0, (SD)=0, continuous measure of weekly hours of TV watching [from P2NUMTV and P2NUMTVW]. Fewer than 1 percent of the sample indicated that there was no TV present in the house.

Number of Rules about TV Watching – Dummy coded measure indicating the presence of several rules regarding TV watching Z-score, 1=at least two rules, 0=one or no rules, from summed composite indicated whether or not there are any family rules about TV watching, rules for how late the child may watch TV, and rules about the number of hours the child may watch TV [from P2TVRULE, P2TVRUL2, P2TVRUL3].

Frequency of Play Activities – Z-score, Mean=0, (SD)=1, factor analytic composite measure of the frequency of various parental at-home play activities (items originally coded from 1=not at all to 4= everyday): play games, build things, do sports, teach child about nature, help child do art, tell stories, sing songs, have child do chores   [from P1GAMES, P1BUILD, P1SPORT, P1NATURE, P1HELPAR, P1TELLST, P1SINGSO, and P1CHORES].

Frequency of Reading Activities – Z-score, Mean=0, (SD)=1, factor analytic composite measure of the frequency of various at-home reading and book-related activities (items originally coded from 1=not at all to 4= everyday): parent reads to child, child looks at picture books outside of school, child reads or pretends to read books outside of school, [from P1CHREAD, P1CHLPIC, P1READBO].

Media [Books &Tapes (high) vs. TV (low)] – Z-score, Mean=0, (SD)=1, factor analytic composite measure of prevalent home media, coded so that a high (positive) score represents a home with many books & many records/ tapes/CDs (and where *Sesame Street* is not regularly watched), and a low (negative) score represents a home with few books & recordings (and where *Sesame Street* is regularly watched) [from P1CHLBOO, P1CHLAUD, P1CHSESA].

Outside-Home (Non-School Activities):

Arts & Crafts Activities – Dummy coded measure indicating out-of-school participation in either art lessons or craft classes or both [from P2ARTCRF and P2CRAFTS].

Educational Trips – Z-score, Mean=0, (SD)=1, from summed composite of the number of out-of-school activities: visits a zoo, visits a museum, visits the library, goes to a play/concert [from P2ZOO, P2MUSEUM, P2LIBRAR, P2CONCRT].

Sports & Clubs – Z-score, Mean=0, (SD)=1, from summed composite of the number of out-of-school activities: participates in athletic events, attends sporting event, participates in organized clubs [from P2ATHLET, P2SPORT, and P2CLUB].

Performing & Creative Arts – Dummy coded measure indicating out-of-school participation in one or more of the following activities: organized performing, dance lessons, music lessons, drama classes [from P2ORGANZ, P2DANCE, P2MUSIC, P2DRAMA].

Measures of School Quality – Social Context:

Entering Cognitive Skill – Aggregate measure of school-average entering achievement (within-school mean of the sum of z-scored versions of the fall math score and the fall literacy score).

Heterogeneity of Entering Cognitive Skill – Aggregate measure of the within-school variability (within-school standard deviation of entering skill).

Average SES – Aggregate measure of school-average SES (within-school mean of student SES).

Heterogeneity of Entering SES – Aggregate measure of the within-school variability (within-school standard deviation of SES).

Measures of School Quality — School Resources:

Kindergarten Class Size – Size of kindergarten class [from teacher survey: summing A1BOYS and A1GIRLS].

General Parental Outreach – Standardized factor analytic composite measure of general school outreach efforts, Mean=0, SD=1. Original items include school administrator's indication of the frequency of: PTA/PTO meetings, classroom programs, news sent home, home visits, performances for parents, fairs or social events, teacher workshops on parent involvement, report cards, parent/teacher conferences [from school administrator survey: S2PTAMT, S2CLASPR, S2NWSHME, S2HVISIT, S2INVITE, S2FUNDSRS, S2WRKSHP, S2RPRTCD, S2PTCONF].

Kindergarten Transition Outreach – Aggregate measure of school-average number of kindergarten transition efforts (with-in school mean of a summed composite). Original items include teachers' indications of the number of special efforts to assist in the transition into kindergarten, including: send information home to parents, preschoolers spend time in kindergarten classrooms, shortened school days at the beginning of the school year, parents and child visiting kindergarten prior to the start of the school year, home visits at the beginning of the school year, parent orientation prior to the start of school [from teacher survey: B1INFOHO, B1INKNDR, B1SHRTN, B1VSTK, B1HMEVST, B1PRNTOR].

Teacher Preparation – Standardized composite measure of teacher preparation, Z-score, Mean=0, SD=1. Includes number of college courses in teaching methods in math and reading, child development, early childhood education, and elementary education, and level of highest degree completed [from teacher survey: B1MTHDMA, B1MTHDRD, B1DEVLP, B1EARLY, B1ELEM, B1HGHSTD].

Teacher Experience – Standardized composite measure of teacher experience, Z-score, Mean=0, SD=1. Includes years taught at this school and years taught kindergarten [from teacher survey: B1YRSCH, B1YRSKIN].

Collective Responsibility – Aggregate measure of school-average teacher perceptions of collective responsibility for teaching (within-school mean of a factor analytic scale). Original items include teacher responses to: teacher would choose teaching again, teacher enjoys present teaching job, teacher can make a difference in children's lives, children incapable of learning (reverse-coded), child misbehavior affects teaching (reverse-coded), and

paperwork interferes with teaching (reverse-coded) [from teacher survey: B1TEACH, B1ENJOY, B1MKDIFF, B1NOTAP, B1MISBHV, B1PAPRWR].

Professional Community – Aggregate measure of school-average teacher perceptions of the school as a professional community (with-in school mean of a factor analytic scale). Original items include teacher responses to: school administrator prioritizes well, school administrator handles outside pressure, school administrator communicates vision, school administrator encourages staff, how much teachers impact policy, staff learn/seek new ideas, staff accept me as a colleague, staff have school spirit [from teacher survey: B1PRIORI, B1PRESSU, B1ALLKNO, B1ENCOUR, B1SCHPLC, B1CNTNLR, B1ACCPTD, B1SCHSPR].

Measures of School Quality — Environment:

Neighborhood Problems Surrounding School – Composite measure describing the neighborhood surrounding the school, averaged across eight items: tension from differences, problems with unkempt areas, problems with substance abuse, problems with gangs, problems with heavy traffic, problems with violent crime, problems with vacant buildings, problems with crime in the area (individual items originally on a scale from 1 = no problem, to 3 = big problem). Collapsed into four categories: (a) none [mean = 1]; (b) slight [$1 <$ mean ≤ 1.5]; (c) small [$1.5 <$ mean < 2]; and (d) somewhat or big [mean ≥ 2] [from school administrator survey: S2TNSION, S2LITTER, S2DRUGS, S2GANGS, S2TRFFIC, S2VLENCE, S2VCANCY, S2CRIME].

Bad Conditions Near School – Composite measure of conditions near school, averaged across four items: litter and trash, graffiti near school, boarded up buildings, and people congregating (individual items originally on a scale from 0 = none to 3 = a lot). Collapsed into three categories: (a) none or slight [mean $\leq .5$], (b) very little [$.5 <$ mean ≤ 1], (b) some or more [mean > 1][from facilities checklist: K2Q3A_A, K2Q3B_B, K2Q3C_C, K2Q3D_D].

Severe Problems Inside School – Sum of the number of severe problems in school (weapons, theft, and attacks). Collapsed to 0 = no problems, 1 = one problem, 2 = two or more problems [from school administrator survey: S2WEAPON, S2FORCE, S2ATTACK].

Endnotes

1.   Phillips, Crouse, and Ralph (1998) report a black/white achievement gap in math for 4th graders of .87 SD, a reading gap of .74 SD using data from the Prospects study. Using NAEP data, the gaps they report were .7-.8 SD. As readers will learn later in the report, the racial/ethnic gaps we find for children entering kindergarten are somewhat smaller than those reported by Phillips and her colleagues. We speculate that racial/ethnic gaps may increase as children move through school for several reasons, including: (1) minority children attend schools that are systematically lower in quality (see Chapter 4 of this report); (2) children's educational experiences in the same school are differentiated by social background; and (3) children's educational attainment may continue to be influenced by out-of-school, home background factors.

2.   In this report, we use the terms "social class," "socioeconomic status," and "SES" inter-changeably. Socioeconomic status, very often abbreviated with SES, is a standard concept in social science research. This concept, and the measure we use to capture it, includes five different components to describe children's family background (all reported by parents either at the fall or spring data collection): (1) father/male guardian's education, (2) mother/female guardian's education; (3) father/male guardian's occupation, (4) mother/female guardian's occupation, and (5) household income. The parents' occupation was recoded to reflect the average of the 1989 General Social Survey prestige score of the occupation (NCES 1999, 7-9). These are the standard components of SES used in social research, according to White (1982), who conducted a meta-analysis of over 200 studies linking SES with academic achievement.

3.   Although the ECLS-K sample of children was meant to be random, about 15% of the original sample children whose home language was other than English (the language of testing) were screened by data collectors with a brief screening test called "OLDS" (Oral Language Development Scale). Sixty-two percent of those whose native language was Spanish were screened; 38% of children with other home languages were screened. Those who passed the OLDS screening were given the full cognitive tests in both reading and math. Those who failed and whose native language was Spanish were given a brief mathematics test in Spanish, but are not included in our sample. All other children who scored below an established cut score on the OLDS language screener, and whose home language was anything other than Spanish were not tested. However, although "[f]ewer than one percent of the total ECLS-K sample were excluded from the direct child assessment..." (NCES 1999, 5-12), of the children whose native language was Spanish, 71% failed the OLDS screening; of those whose native language was other than Spanish or English, 29% failed the OLDS screening (NCES 1999, Table 5-1).

Because these screening criteria differentially affected Hispanic and Asian children, the samples of children from these two racial/ethnic groups in our analyses are likely to be somewhat more selective than the population from which they were drawn. Although the weights supplied with the ECLS-K data were meant to correct sample sizes for this differential loss, the Hispanic and Asian child samples themselves are not

entirely representative of children of those ethnicities who attend U.S. kindergartens. For example, other analyses we conducted found that of Hispanic children from non-English speaking homes, only 33% had full cognitive test data (and would, thus, be part of our analyses). For Asian children from non-English homes, only 48% have cognitive test data. Besides race/ethnicity and non-English speaking household, we also found that higher SES children has a higher probability of having full test data. Non-English households in the U.S. are of lower SES.

4.   We argue that the ECLS-K data are extremely useful for addressing the issues raised in this report. The major value of a study like ECLS-K inheres from two strengths: (1) researchers' ability to generalize findings, because of the large and nationally representative sample of children and schools, and (2) the longitudinal nature of the data (not explored in this report). For studying the national distribution of school and classroom structures in the kindergarten year or exploring policy issues relevant to kindergarten, such as whether children learn more in full-day or half-day programs, the data structure seems very strong. This will also apply to other elementary-school grades, as further waves of ECLS-K data become available.

On the other hand, any general-purpose data collection effort inherently has shortcomings. For example, the broad scope of its purpose means that within ECLS-K any particular issue is captured by only a small number of survey items that are seldom adequate to address such issues in depth. Another example of a shortcoming is the difficulty of capturing a complete picture of children's care and preschool experiences the year before kindergarten (e.g., we don't even know whether particular care arrangements had any academic content, how long the children were in these care settings, the qualifications and numbers of staff, or the adequacy of the facilities). The survey items about home environment are also limited; although they capture the presence or absence of particular resources, practices or activities, they provide little information about their quality. As stated, such shortcomings are inherent in any general purpose study. Thus, a thorough study of many of the issues covered in ECLS-K would require more focused and in-depth surveys or qualitative studies in a few settings. Of course, such studies would not yield the generalizability of ECLS-K, and would also seldom follow children for several years.

5.   Some readers may feel it is appropriate to account for "design effects" into statistical testing, although we have not adjusted our levels of statistical testing for this type of clustering. Design effects differ for individual variables (and groups of children), and refer to the underestimation of the standard errors leading to more liberal significance testing. The impact of these design effects is seen most severely with descriptive and bivariate results. In multivariate settings (like multiple regression with many predictors), the impact is usually quite modest. To compensate, some readers may want to regard our statistical tests (especially those in Tables 2.1 and 2.2) more conservatively, by "subtracting" one asterisk from each statistical test. That is, differences identified as statistically significant at probability levels of .001 or below (indicated with three asterisks) might be dropped to a probability level below .01. In most cases, differences indicated as statistically significant will not drop below the conventional probability level: $p < .05$.

6.   We have normalized these weights (i.e., performed a linear adjustment so the weights will average 1), in order to preserve the sample sizes in the ECLS-K data file for appropriate statistical testing.

7.   We recognize that the "other" racial category is not distinctive and thus lacks precision of meaning that adheres to the other racial/ethnic categories. However, we retain this separate group in our analysis for two important reasons: (1) the ECLS-K is a nationally representative study, so that eliminating one racial group would no longer retain this important advantage; and (2) were we to fold the "other" group into the comparison (white children), the comparison would lose its distinctiveness. In other words, the only way to estimate correctly the black/white gap is to pull out the "other" group into a separate category. Moreover, the very small proportions of the Native American and self-identified mixed-race groups in the population preclude their separate analysis. Thus, our treatment of this group seems a reasonable compromise. As a result, we tend not to make much of the "other"/white differences. In addition, our choice of whites as the fixed reference group is fairly arbitrary, mostly reflecting the fact that they are the largest subgroup. We make no evaluative judgment by this choice. Finally, we wish to acknowledge that these large racial and ethnic categories by no means define homogeneous populations. All these groups display substantial diversity within the categories. That said, educators and policy makers justifiably continue to investigate such average group differences as one general measure of societal success with equalizing the distribution of opportunities and resources.

8.   Though the information about the large majority of these activities and home environmental factors was drawn from parental reports collected in surveys administered at the beginning of the kindergarten year, parents were only asked about outside-of-home activities in the survey collected at the end of the kindergarten year. Thus, for reports of outside activities, we admit to the possibility that the frequency of these activities might be influenced by the kindergarten experience (or change over the year) and hence not precisely reflect only "starting gate" experiences. Our decision to use parental reports of such activities in this report was predicated on a desire not to overlook a substantial literature about the importance of cultural capital in children's intellectual development.

9.   Recall that the language screening described in endnote 3 eliminated some children who were considered to be unable to participate in the cognitive testing. The sample for our analyses in this report is restricted to ECLS-sampled children with cognitive test scores at kindergarten entry. Thus, the proportion of children living in non-English households is somewhat underestimated here. Therefore, these are the children in our sample in such households who themselves speak English well enough to have passed the screening test and participate in the testing.

10.   There are several reasons why children might repeat kindergarten, although such information is not available in ECLS-K. Children may be immature in terms of behavior, or they may not demonstrate adequate skills to allow them to take advantage of academic instruction.

11.   Of course, these analyses are cross-sectional only, so causal direction is unclear. Whether income goes down as a result of family disruption or whether less advantaged individuals are more likely to become single parents is unknown. However, there is considerable evidence that the family income of women caring for children alone plummets after a divorce. We have not included here the proportions of single-parent households that result from divorce, separation, death, or whether the single parent was never married, although such information is available in ECLS-K.

12. Information about ECLS-K children's Head Start attendance before kindergarten is very accurate. For parents who indicated that their children had attended Head Start, the center's name and location were requested and verified (NCES 2002b). Thus, we know that all children in the Head Start category actually had a preschool experience (though whether it was a full-day or a half-day program is not known). For children whose parents indicated that the child had attended center-based childcare, there is no information about the program's content.

13. In step 3, we also include a measure that captures how far into the school year the tests were administered. We draw no particular meaning from this variable; rather, it takes into account the fact that many children actually experienced some schooling by testing time. It is often the case that achievement testing that is meant to be administered at the beginning or end of a school year actually extends into the school year at either end. The point here is to adjust for the amount of time these children actually spent in kindergarten, as our focus is on their cognitive status at the very start of school.

14. As mentioned, we recognize that the analyses in this entire report, but particularly those described in this chapter, present some difficulty. That is, the analyses are cross-sectional (i.e., all the measures were collected more at less at the same time). That means that we are not in a good position to infer causality. Relationships shown in the entire report are correlational. However, we do make use of the phrase "effect size" frequently in the report, particularly in Chapters 3 and 4, a common practice in discussing regression-based research of this sort. When we use the OLS regression technique, where variables are either "dependent" or "independent," talking about the "effect" of variable X on variable Y is customary. Although we use the language of "effects," we recognize that our ability to infer "cause" is weak.

15. Although the R^2 values we report on Table 3.2 are unadjusted for the large number of variables in our models, the adjusted R^2 values are almost identical to the unadjusted values. This is because the sample size is very large, and the ratio of number of cases to number of independent variables is also quite high.

16. This is a continuous measure, representing the simple ratio of family income to family size, anchored so that a needs ratio of "1" indicates that his or her family income is exactly at the poverty level, a ratio of "2" is twice that income. Thus, a higher number on this variable represents a higher family income (and less need).

17. In general, the measures of school quality are school-level or classroom-level variables, constructed either by aggregating information about children (from test scores or parent surveys) or taken directly from information about teachers and schools supplied by surveys of these individuals. The school-level and teacher-level variables were appended to child-level information, and the analyses were conducted at the level of individual children. Because the samples for each school quality analysis vary somewhat, based on the availability of outcome data for each school, child sample sizes for each analysis are reported in Tables 4.1-4.3.

18. The log-odds metric is in many ways an unintuitive one, but certain characteristics of the metric are easy to understand. A zero (or non-significant change) in the log-odds indicates that the likelihood of enrolling in a private (as opposed to public) school is not affected by this characteristic of the child. A positive change in the log-odds indicates that a certain characteristic is associated with a greater likelihood of enrolling in a private school; a negative change in the log-odds indicates that the characteristic is

associated with a lesser likelihood of enrolling in a private school. One can also transform the log-odds metric into the odds metric by the following equation: odds = $e^{(\log\text{-odds})}$. Hence, a .70 change in the log-odds (i.e., an increased likelihood) is equivalent to an $e^{(.70)}$) = 2.01 change in the odds. This represents a 101% increase, in the odds of enrolling in a private school, thus doubling the odds. A -.40 change in log-odds (i.e., a decreased likelihood) is equivalent to an $e^{(-.40)}$ = -0.67 change in the odds. This represents a 33% decrease in the odds of enrolling in a private school.

19. The ECLS-K data include many other measures that may be interpreted as "resources," including those associated with kindergarten classrooms and the instructional methods used by teachers. Because our array of resource measures is already quite broad and our analyses are targeted at the entry point, we chose to limit measures of quality that were both different from one another and around which many people would agree. Most importantly, the major purpose of our analyses in this chapter is to capture school quality with a wide array of measures, rather than capture each and every one.

20. Although many of the socioeconomic differences in access to school quality are smaller than those seen in Chapters 1-3, it is important to remember that in Chapter 4 we have split apart this construct into three constituent pieces (poverty status or needs ratio, parents' education, and parents' occupational prestige). Given that these various components of SES are correlated, and that multivariate techniques are designed to estimate the *net effect* of any one predictor independent of all others, the unique impact each separate piece is bound to be much smaller than the effect when all are combined into a single measure.

Bibliography

Alexander, K.L. & Entwisle, D.R. (1989). Achievement in the first 2 years of school: Patterns and processes. *Mongraphs of the Society for Research in Child Development*, *53*(2), Serial No. 218.

Applebee, A.N., Langer, J.A., & Mullis, I. (1988). *Who reads best? Factors relating to reading achievement in grades 3, 7, and 11*. Princeton, NJ: Educational Testing Service.

Brooks-Gunn, J., Duncan, G., & Britto, P. (1999) Are socioeconomic gradients for children similar to those for adults? In D. Keating & C. Hertzman (Eds.), *Developmental health and the wealth of nations* (pp. 94-124). New York: The Guilford Press.

Bryk, A.S. & Lee, V.E. (1992). Is politics the problem and markets the answer? An essay review of Politics, Markets, and America's Schools. *Economics of Education Review*, *11*(4), 439-451.

Case, R., Griffin, S., & Kelley, W. (1999). Socioeconomic gradients in mathematical ability and their responsiveness to intervention during early childhood. In D. Keating & C. Hertzman (Eds.), *Developmental health and the wealth of nations* (pp. 125-149). New York: The Guilford Press.

Cusick, P.A. (1983). *The egalitarian ideal and the American high school*. New York: Longman.

Entwisle, D.R., Alexander, K.L., & Olson, L.S. (1997). *Children, schools, and inequality*. Boulder, CO: Westview.

Fantini, M.D. & Weinstein, G. (1968). *The disadvantaged: Challenge to education*. New York: Harper and Row.

General Accounting Office (GAO) (2001 April). *Early childhood programs: The use of impact evaluations to assess program effects*. Washington, DC: Government Printing Office, GAO-01-542.

Hart, B. & Risley, T.R. (1995). *Meaningful differences in the everyday experience of young American children*. Baltimore: Paul H. Brookes Publishing Company.

Huttenlocher, J.E., Haiaght, W., Bryk, A.S., & Seltzer, M. Early vocabulary growth: Relation to language input and gender. *Developmental Psychology*. *27*(2), 236-249.

Jencks, C. & Phillips, M. (1998). The black/white test score gap: An introduction. In C. Jencks & M. Phillips (Eds.). *The black/white Test Score Gap* (pp. 1-51). Washington, DC: Brookings.

Keating, D.P. & Hertzman, C. (1999). *Developmental health and the wealth of nations*. New York: The Guilford Press.

Lee, V.E. (1993). Educational choice: The stratifying effects of selecting schools and courses. *Educational Policy, 7*(2), 125-148.

Lee, V.E., Burkam, D.T., Honigman, J.J., & Meisels, S.J. (2001). *Full-day vs. half-day kindergarten: Which children learn more in which program?* Paper presented at the annual meeting of the American Sociological Association, Anaheim, CA, August 2001.

Lee, V.E., Croninger, R.G., & Smith, J.B. (1994). Parental choice of schools and social stratification in education: The paradox of Detroit. *Educational Evaluation and Policy Analysis, 16*(4), 434-457.

Lee, V.E. & Loeb, S. (2000). School size in Chicago elementary schools: Effects on teachers' attitudes and students' achievement. *American Educational Research Journal, 37*(1), 3-31.

Lee, V.E. & Smith, J.B. (1996). Collective responsibility for learning and its effects on gains in achievement for early secondary school students. *American Journal of Education, 104*(2), 103-147.

Louis, K.S., Kruse, S.D., & Marks, H.M. (1996a). Schoolwide professional community (pp. 179-204). In F.M. Newmann and Associates. *Authentic achievement: Restructuring schools for intellectual quality.* San Francisco: Jossey-Bass.

Louis, K.S., Marks, H.M., and Kruse, S. (1996b). Teachers' professional community in restructuring schools. *American Educational Research Journal, 33*(4), 757-798.

McKee, R.H., Dondelli, L., Ganson, H., Barrett, B.J., McDonkey, C., & Plantz, M.C. (1985 June). *The impact of head start on chlidren, families, and communities.* Final report of the Head Start evaluation, synthesis, and utilization project. Washington, DC: U.S. Government Printing Office, DHHS Publication No. (OHDS) 85-31193.

National Center for Education Statistics (1999 August). *ECLS-K data user's manual.* Washington, DC: U.S. Department of Education, Office of Educational Research and Improvement (NCES 2000-070).

National Center for Education Statistics (2000a January). *America's kindergartners.* Washington, DC: U.S. Department of Education, Office of Educational Research and Improvement (NCES 2000-070).

National Center for Education Statistics (2000b). *ECLS-K base year data files and electronic codebook.* Washington, DC: U.S. Department of Education, Office of Educational Research and Improvement.

Phillips, M., Brooks-Gunn, J., Duncan, G.J., Klebanov, P., & Crane, J. (1998). Family background, parenting practices, and the black/white test score gap. In C. Jencks & M. Phillips (Eds.). *The black/white Test Score Gap* (pp. 103-145). Washington, DC: Brookings.

Phillips, M., Crouse, J., & Ralph, J. (1998). Does the black/white test score gap widen after children enter school? In C. Jencks & M. Phillips (Eds.). *The black/white Test Score Gap* (pp. 229-272). Washington, DC: Brookings.

Rosenthal, R. & Rosnow, R.L. (1984). *Essentials of behavioral research: Methods and data analysis*. New York: McGraw-Hill.

Stipek, D.J & Ryan, R.R. (1997). Economically disadvantaged preschoolers: Ready to learn but further to go. *Developmental Psychology, 33*, 711-723.

Snow, C.E., Burns, M.S., & Griffin, P. (Eds). (1998). *Preventing reading difficulties in young children*. Washington, DC: National Academy Press.

White, K.R. 1982. The relationship between socioeconomic status and academic achievement. *Psychological Bulletin*, 91, 461-481.

Willms, J.D. 1999. Quality and inequality in children's literacy: The effects of families, schools and communities. In D. Keating & C.Hertzman, eds., *Developmental health and the wealth of nations* (pp. 72-93). New York: The Guilford Press.

About EPI

The Economic Policy Institute was founded in 1986 to widen the debate about policies to achieve healthy economic growth, prosperity, and opportunity.

Today, despite a recent period of rapid growth in the U.S. economy, inequality in wealth, wages, and income remains historically high. Expanding global competition, changes in the nature of work, and rapid technological advances are altering economic reality. Yet many of our policies, attitudes, and institutions are based on assumptions that no longer reflect real world conditions.

With the support of leaders from labor, business, and the foundation world, the Institute has sponsored research and public discussion of a wide variety of topics: trade and fiscal policies; trends in wages, incomes, and prices; education; the causes of the productivity slowdown; labor market problems; rural and urban policies; inflation; state-level economic development strategies; comparative international economic performance; and studies of the overall health of the U.S. manufacturing sector and of specific key industries.

The Institute works with a growing network of innovative economists and other social science researchers in universities and research centers all over the country who are willing to go beyond the conventional wisdom in considering strategies for public policy.

Founding scholars of the Institute include Jeff Faux, EPI president; Lester Thurow, Sloan School of Management, MIT; Ray Marshall, former U.S. secretary of labor, professor at the LBJ School of Public Affairs, University of Texas; Barry Bluestone, University of Massachusetts-Boston; Robert Reich, former U.S. secretary of labor; and Robert Kuttner, author, editor of *The American Prospect,* and columnist for *Business Week* and the Washington Post Writers Group.

For additional information about the Institute, contact EPI at 1660 L Street NW, Suite 1200, Washington, DC 20036, (202) 775-8810, or visit www.epinet.org.